PRICELESS STONES

42 Days of Hebrew Promises for Kingdom Living

James Revoir

Priceless Stones

CrossLink Publishing
www.crosslinkpublishing.com

Copyright, © 2013 James Revoir

All rights reserved. No part of this book may be reproduced in any form, except for brief quotations in reviews, without the written permission of the author.

Printed in the United States of America. All rights reserved under International Copyright Law.

ISBN 978-1-936746-37-8

Taken from *Basics of Biblical Hebrew Grammar* by Gary D. Pratico and Miles V. Van Pelt. Copyright © 2001 by Zondervan. Use by permission of Zondervan. www.zondervan.com

The Brown-Driver-Briggs Hebrew and English Lexicon by F Brown, S. Driver, and C. Briggs, copyright 2003 by Hendrickson Publishers, Peabody, Massachusetts. Used by permission. All rights reserved.

Commentary on the Old Testament, Volume I. C. F. Keil and F. Delitzsch, copyright 1996 by Hendrickson Publishers, Peabody, Massachusetts. Used by permission. All rights reserved.

Taken from *The Expositor's Bible Commentary, Vol. II* by Walter C. Kaiser, Jr.. Copyright © 1990 by Zondervan. Use by permission of Zondervan. www.zondervan.com

Taken from *The IVP BIble Background Commentary: Old Testament* by John H. Walton, Victor H. Matthews and Mark W. Chavalas.

Copyright(c) 2000 by John H. Walton, Victor H. Matthews and Mark W. Chavalas. Used by permission of InterVarsity Press, PO Box 1400, Downers Grove, IL 60515. www.ivpress.com

Taken from *Judges & Ruth, An Introduction & Commentary* by Arthur E. Cundall and Leon Morris. Copyright(c) 1968 by Arthur E. Cundall and Leon Morris. Used by permission of InterVarsity Press, PO Box 1400, Downers Grove, IL 60515. www.ivpress.com

Scripture taken from the NEW AMERICAN STANDARD BIBLE(r), (c) Copyright 1960, 1962, 1963, 1968, 1971, 1972, 1973, 1975, 1977, 1995 by The Lockman Foundation Used by permission." (www.Lockman.org)

Taken from *New International Dictionary of Old Testament Theology & Exegesis, Volume 1* by Willem A. VanGemeren, Copyright © 1997 by Zondervan. Use by permission of Zondervan. www.zondervan.com

Taken from *New International Dictionary of Old Testament Theology & Exegesis, Volume 3* by Willem A. VanGemeren, Copyright © 1977 by Zondervan. Use by permission of Zondervan. www.zondervan.com

Taken from *New International Dictionary of Old Testament Theology & Exegesis, Volume 4* by Willem A. VanGemeren, Copyright © 1991 by Zondervan. Use by permission of Zondervan. www.zondervan.com

Taken from *New International Dictionary of Old Testament Theology & Exegesis, Volume 5* by Willem A. VanGemeren, Copyright © 1991 by Zondervan. Use by permission of Zondervan. www.zondervan.com

Scripture taken from the New King James Version®. Copyright © 1982 by Thomas Nelson, Inc. Used by permission. All rights reserved.

Taken from *The Strongest Strong's Exhaustive Concordance of the Bible* by James Strong. Copyright © 2001 by Zondervan. Use by permission of Zondervan. www.zondervan.com

Taken from *Trusting Thy Word* by James T. Draper Jr. Copyright (c) 1989 by Broadman Press. Reprinted and used by permission.

DEDICATION

To my Dad and Mom and my precious sisters, Jackie and Julie

ACKNOWLEDGEMENTS

Brian and Lindsay Moore and Tree of Life Church: Thank you for pouring so much of yourselves into my life and showing me, through your lives, the passionate love of the Father, His Son Jesus Christ, and Holy Spirit and what it truly means to live in union with Them.

Mahlon and Juanita Stone: Thank you for taking me into your home and sustaining me at a very low point in my life.

Aundrae Kincaid: Thank you for loving me into the Kingdom when the rest of the world had discarded me. You are truly missed but I'll see you again and thank you a million times over on that glorious Day!

TABLE OF CONTENTS

DAY 1 1
He Alone Empowers Us to Love Him
Deuteronomy 6:4-5

DAY 2 5
Red As Scarlet, White As Snow
Isaiah 1:18

DAY 3 9
He Is Our Wonderful Security Blanket!
Psalm 91:1

DAY 4 13
Direction Comes through Deep Intimacy with God
Proverbs 3:5-6

DAY 5 17
The Lord Surrounds Us with His Protective Favor
Psalm 5:12

DAY 6 21
A Personal Invitation to Biblical Meditation
Joshua 1:8

DAY 7 26
The Voice of the Lord Is Like Thunder
Psalm 29:3

DAY 8 30
Blessing Our Parents with Heavy Honor
Exodus 20:12

DAY 9 34
God's Free Gift to You Is His Holy Nature
Leviticus 20:26

DAY 10 38
Almond Joy
Numbers 17:8

DAY 11 41
You Have Been Personally Handmade by God
Genesis 2:7

DAY 12 45
We Are One with Our Spouse and One with Christ
Genesis 2:24

DAY 13 49
His Name Is Gloriously Wonderful!
Judges 13:18

DAY 14 53
His Word Lights My Path
Psalm 119:105

DAY 15 57
The Desirable Fear of the Lord
Proverbs 1:7

DAY 16 61
God Is Really, Really Excited over Us!
Zephaniah 3:17

DAY 17 66
He Is the Mighty, Mighty God
Psalm 24:7-8

DAY 18 70
He Miraculously Saves Us
Psalm 145:19

DAY 19 73
He Is Our Abundant Peace
Numbers 6:26

DAY 20 76
The Rope of Hope
Jeremiah 29:11

DAY 21 81
His Mercy Endures Forever
Psalm 136:1

DAY 22 86
He Is the Amazing I AM
Exodus 3:14

DAY 23 91
He Is Our Provider
Genesis 22:14

DAY 24 96
He Is Our Healer
Exodus 15:26

DAY 25 100
Wherever You Are, He Is There
Ezekiel 48:35

DAY 26 103
He Is Our Victorious Banner
Exodus 17:15

DAY 27 107
He Is the Mighty Lord of Hosts
1 Samuel 17:45

DAY 28 111
He Is Our Freely-Given Righteousness
Jeremiah 23:5-6

DAY 29 117
The Lord Alone Is Faithful to Keep His Covenant
Genesis 17:7

DAY 30 123
We Are God's One-of-a-Kind Treasure
Exodus 19:5

DAY 31 129
Fatness Is in the Eye of the Beholder
Isaiah 55:2

DAY 32 132
We Are God's Olive Trees
Jeremiah 11:16

DAY 33 137
Creepy, Crawly Things
Ezekiel 8:10

DAY 34 143
Never Left, Never Forsaken
Joshua 1:5

DAY 35 148
How to Outshine the Frogs and the Crickets
Psalm 150:6

DAY 36 152
He Loves Us with a Passionate Jealousy
Exodus 34:14

DAY 37 155
We Are Clean, Shiny and Pure!
Exodus 36:25-26

DAY 38 161
Amazing Suffering, Amazing Healing, Amazing Love!
Isaiah 53:4

DAY 39 166
The Ultimate Disappearing Act
Genesis 5:24

DAY 40 171
He Reveals His Secret to Those Who Love Him
Psalm 25:14

DAY 41 176
Our Spouse Is More than a Sidekick
Genesis 2:18

DAY 42 181
We Are the Apple of His Eye
Zechariah 2:8

English-Hebrew Glossary 189

Hebrew-English Glossary 193

Scripture Index 197

Bibliography 203

Endnotes 211

DAY 1

מאד

m^{e}od

He Alone Empowers Us to Love Him

Hear, O Israel: The Lord our God is one Lord: And thou shalt love the Lord thy God with all thine heart, and with all thy soul, and with all thy might.
— Deuteronomy 6:4-5[1]

Too often, we tend to divide our lives into segments which belong to different people. The daytime hours of Monday through Friday may belong to our job or school; the evening hours and weekends may belong to our family; and depending on our religious faith or denomination, Saturday or Sunday morning may belong to God. How many times have we heard people say that what a person does behind closed doors does not affect how he or she does his job—especially when it comes to those holding a political office? The truth is, at all times, God desires nothing less than our undivided love. He does not distinguish between our work life, our school life, our family life, our religious life, etc.

In Jewish culture, hearing, listening, and obeying are one and the same–they are inseparable; hence, the same verb *sh^{e}ma* includes all three actions.[2] Hearing is passive; listening is active; and obedience is responsive. If you have not obeyed, then you have not really heard. Deuteronomy 6:4-9, beginning with the imperative "Hear!" is known as the *Sh^{e}ma*. It is the supreme confession of the Jewish faith.

To put these verses in context, the Book of Deuteronomy was given to Moses in the form of a legal covenant between God and

Israel. This covenant was established at the end of Israel's wilderness wanderings, just as the Israelites were about to enter the Promised Land. During the time when this was established, it was common for a powerful king to establish such an agreement with a weaker nation or kingdom which he had conquered. This was called a *suzerain-vassal* agreement.

In this case, the King was the Lord, and the subject was Israel. The Lord had delivered the entire nation of Israel from slavery in Egypt by supernatural wonders and had faithfully provided for their every need for nearly forty years. Now, He was promising to give the Israelites the land which He had promised to their forefathers Abraham, Isaac, and Jacob. The Lord did all these things, not because the Israelites deserved them—for they had complained incessantly—but He did so purely out His grace and mercy.

All of us, if we think long and hard enough, can think of things which others have done for us which we have not deserved—the policeman who let us off with a warning when we knew we had been speeding and were expecting a ticket; the teacher who gave us a passing grade when we should have failed; the friend who gave us money when we could not pay the rent; and the list goes on and on…What is our natural response? Why, gratitude, of course, and love for that person! How much more should we love God, who has done more for us than we will ever know? He has created us; He has protected us; He has provided for us; and above all, He has given us grace and mercy which we did not deserve.

The greatest command which the Lord gives us is the law of love. The love which the Lord commands of us in Deuteronomy 6:5 is total in nature. We are to love the Lord with all our heart, soul, and our might. The Hebrew word m^eod, translated "might" is an adverb meaning *exceedingly, abundantly*, or, at the risk of using poor English, *with muchness* or *force*.[3] This love is far from being a passive emotion; rather, it is all-consuming, from the deepest core of our being! Biblical love, be it love for God or love for others, goes beyond emotions. It is expressed on three levels—through our emotions, through our words, and through our actions. If any one of these is missing, our love is incomplete.

Have you ever noticed how athletes sometimes scream out during some sporting events? Often this is seen during weightlifting or field events during the Olympics or when tennis players swing the tennis racket at Wimbledon. They do not scream to simply make a noise, but to draw out every fiber of strength that is in them. Considering all that the Lord has done for us, ought not our love for Him be no less deliberate, no less visible, and no less intense? When we think of how much we have fallen short of this seemingly impossible standard, it can be very discouraging. The encouraging news is that God already knows this and He understands our weakness. Jesus said, "For without me ye can do nothing (John 15:5)." Through the prism of our human pride, we read this verse and water it down to mean that we can do "nothing of spiritual Significance"—in other words, we presume that there are some things we can do in our own strength but that there are other areas where we need His special help. No! No! No! In the New Testament text, the Greek word for "nothing" means *nothing*-absolutely *nothing*! We are incapable of even loving Him unless He empowers us to do so. He does through the power of His Holy Spirit who comes to live inside of us. Do you want to love God? Of course you do because this is the very reason for which we were created! Give the Lord Jesus Christ your heart; but even more so, give Him your frail human weakness and watch Him ignite in you a flaming passion for Him that you have never known or experienced! *He wants to do it and He longs to do it! All we need to do is ask!*

PRAYER

Lord Jesus, I acknowledge that I have come to the end of myself and my human ability. Please do a supernatural work in me by filling me to overflowing with an overflowing love for You, so that when I meditate on all the things which You have done for me, I cannot help but love You passionately with all my heart, and all my soul, and all my strength. Continue to show me Your goodness and mercy in my life, that I might love You with the same love with which You first loved me. Let my passionate love for You flow to others as well, that they, too, might experience Your goodness and love toward them.

I pray this in the wonderful name of Jesus!

DECLARATION

I declare that by faith, my love for God is all-consuming, everyday. By the power of the Holy Spirit who lives in me, I daily choose by an act of faith to love the Lord with all my heart, with all my soul, and with all my might. I choose to not only love Him with my emotions, but to express my love for Him through my words and songs of praise, and to live out that love through my life, passionately loving Him and passionately loving others. Only He can do it and only He will do it.

I declare this by faith in Jesus' name!

QUESTIONS

1. What do you think it looks like to truly love God?
2. Have you truly come to the end of yourself and your natural ability to love Him as He desires? What is keeping you from surrendering your weakness to Him?
3. What are some of the amazing acts of kindness and mercy that the Lord has shown toward you? Do you thank Him regularly?

DAY 2

דם

dam

Red As Scarlet, White As Snow

Come now, and let us reason together, saith the Lord: though your sins be as scarlet, they shall be as white as snow; though they be red like crimson, they shall be as wool.
– Isaiah 1:18

Have you ever had a leaky pen that got all over your hands, or worse yet, that stained your clothing? Often, even the best of stain removers will still leave a faded spot. I remember an old daytime television commercial that touted a laundry detergent so powerful, it could even remove bloodstains. Bloodstains are notoriously difficult to wash out. Criminals often try feverishly to scrub bloodstains from the crime scenes with the hope of hiding their deeds, only to have them revealed under the glare of infrared light. In a spiritual sense, all of us have been marred by the stain of sin. Even if we manage to hide our imperfections from the rest of the world, our guilt cannot be hid from the infrared, penetrating eyes of an all-knowing God.

    In the book of Isaiah, the Lord was pleading with the Israelites of the Southern Kingdom to return to Him with their whole hearts. Their brothers in the Northern Kingdom had already been carried off into captivity by the brutal Assyrians, and now they were on the verge of likewise being conquered by the Babylonians. In Isaiah 1:18, through the use of contrasting imagery, the Lord was promising the Israelites that, in spite of their idolatry and rebellion against Him, He would still completely cleanse their sins regardless of how heinous they were.

The utter depravity of the Israelites' sins was illustrated by an allusion to deep, scarlet-colored dyes which were well-known at that time for their indelible permanence.[4] One of the Hebrew words for "red" or "crimson" used in this verse is *yadimu,* the third person, plural, future form of the Hebrew verbs *adom* or *adem,* either of which can be translated to mean, "They shall emit or show redness; or, they shall be glaring or flagrant."[5] Embedded in this verb is the root word *dam,* which is the Hebrew word for blood.[6]

As I meditate on this, I am taken back to a time several years ago when I was sharing Christ with a Vietnam veteran. Sadly, he could not bring himself to believe that he could ever be forgiven of his sins because of some things that he had done during the war. The truth is, all of us, whether or not we have physically taken a life, have blood on our hands. All of us stand guilty of sin before God, for the Scripture says, "For all have sinned, and come short of the glory of God" (Romans 3:23).

Ironically, the only antidote to cleanse the blood of our sins is blood itself—not our sinful, contaminated blood—but the pure, sinless blood of the Lord Jesus Christ which He shed on the cross. The old hymn proclaims, "Oh the blood of Jesus, it washes white as snow." The Lord is not content to simply return us to a neutral state of not having sinned—He wants to give us His righteousness in its place. The word used for "white" in this verse is *yalbinu,* meaning, "They shall be made white."[7] A parallel image is found in Psalm 51:9. The root verb is *laban,* which is also the root word embedded in the place name of Lebanon. Historians and linguists believe the region was so named because of its white, snowy, mountain peaks.

Deep in the heart of every person is a longing to be pure. Why else do brides prefer to wear white on their wedding day? What purer purity can we have than that which Christ freely offers to those who put their trust in Him? In 2 Corinthians 5:21, the Apostle Paul declares, "For he hath made him to be sin for us, who knew no sin; that we might be made the righteousness of God in him." The Lord Jesus Christ paid the price in full for every sin of every human being-past, present, and future. Regardless of what we have done, Jesus extends His open arms of forgiveness to us if we will only ask. Jesus promised in John 6:37, "All that the Father giveth me shall come to me; and him that cometh to me I will in no wise cast out." He invites us to not only stand legally forgiven, but to experience the sensation of being completely cleansed! Have you ever known what it feels like to be absolutely clean and pure before God? He invites you and calls you to His unspotted, unblemished purity today! *Give Him your deepest, darkest sins, and He will give you His whitest, brightest purity!*

PRAYER

Lord Jesus, I come to You today, having been tainted with sin. Cleanse my thoughts, cleanse my words, cleanse my actions, and make me whiter than snow. Thank You for Your precious blood which You so freely poured out in my place to pay for all of my sins. I receive Your forgiveness now. Fill me with Your Spirit and flood me with Your righteousness. Thank you for Your never-ending fountain of grace, mercy, and loving-kindness.

I pray this in name of Jesus!

DECLARATION

I declare that I am the righteousness of God in Christ Jesus. I reject shame, guilt, and condemnation. Jesus took all of my sin upon Himself. In exchange He gave me His righteousness, His holiness, and His purity. I have been made a child of God through faith in the Lord Jesus Christ. I choose as an act of my faith to see myself clothed in His righteousness every single day.

I declare this by faith in Jesus' name!

QUESTIONS

1. Have you received the gift of salvation which Christ purchased for you on the cross?
2. Are there any sins which have continued to plague you with shame? Have you confessed them and given them to Christ?
3. What does the Bible say about your identity in Christ? Are you soaking yourself in the promises which He has declared over you in His Word?

DAY 3

עֶלְיוֹן

elyon

He Is Our Wonderful Security Blanket!

He that dwelleth in the secret place of the most High shall abide under the shadow of the Almighty.
– Psalm 91:1

We have all been scared at times in our lives. When I was a child, there was a tree outside of my window which used to cast some very strange shadows on the walls of my bedroom at night. Added to that, every little creak in the house would become magnified in my paranoid little mind to the point that I would instinctively hide under my covers and bury my face under my pillow. Looking back, I think about how God could have made us strong, independent creatures, but chose instead to create us as fragile human beings, wholly dependent upon Him. Young or old, when we face fear, we naturally seek to physically protect ourselves from danger. In the Bible, the rebellious souls in the book of Revelation find themselves hiding in caves and crying out that the rocks might fall on them, out of fear at the coming of the Lord (Revelation 6:15-17).

Like a young child who clings to his favorite blanket, we seek to find comfort in things that cannot ultimately help us. For some, it may be a large home or an expensive car; for others, it may be some sort of escapism or fantasy; and moreover for other people it may come in the form of habits or vices that provide temporary relief like smoking or overeating. In a world of real danger, however, we need real security, and what higher security can there be than to take refuge in the Most High God, who is the Creator of all and Lord over all?

Psalm 91:1 describes one who is continually dwelling or living under the shadow of the Most High God. The title for God is *Elyon*, who is the absolute Highest God in the entire universe.[8] There is no god who is His equal; there is no god who can even come close to His majesty; and there is certainly no god who is higher or greater than He. The Scripture promises that the person who takes refuge in Him shall dwell or abide in the shadow of the Almighty. The word for "shadow" would have had special meaning to the original nomadic audience. This word is *tsel,* also translated "shade." In Israel and the surrounding desert nations of the Middle East, the summer heat can be unbearable, even by midmorning. Job 7:2, describing the harshness of life, alludes to a servant who "earnestly desireth the shadow." Without the relief of shade, there is a very real danger of one dying from heat stroke. Jonah 4:6 relates how God provided a gourd over Jonah to give him relief from the heat of the sun.[9]

In the ancient world, the kings of Mesopotamia and Egypt likened themselves to shadows of protection, not only over their own people, but in their conquering ambitions, over the entire world. Many of us have seen the old Roman and Egyptian movies with the servants waving palm branches over the king or queen. The "frond bearer" came to be a coveted position of status in the royal court; moreover, there was an expression in Mesopotamia that stepping into the shadow of the king was a symbol of receiving privilege, and even receiving a generous financial compensation.[10]

The second half of Psalm 91:1 refers to the Lord as *Shadday*, the Almighty. The root word of *shadday* carries two distinct meanings, both of which reveal God's tender-loving care for those who belong to Him. First, *shad* or *shod* are Hebrew words for the female breast.[11] This illustrates the Lord's abundant provision, as a mother cares for her children. Second, the verb *shadad* carries the idea of ruining, devastating, or violently destroying.[12] On the surface, these qualities might appear to be contradictory, but they actually fit quite well together. Think of how loving and protective many animals are toward their young. Bear cubs found in the wild can be adorable, but it is best to leave the cub alone because the mama bear is always nearby and gets very angry with people who bother her baby! In the same way, the Lord provides for His own children with intimate care and security, generously blessing, with lavish, abundant provision, those who love Him—but woe to those who come against His covenant people! Whose side are you on? Are you under the *"shad*ow" of His grace? If you are not certain about where you stand in your relationship with the Lord, He stands ever ready to bring you under the shadow of His warm, protective wings. He does not want you to dwell in fear any longer, but to know beyond the "shadow" of a doubt that you are His child! He will never, ever leave you to fend for yourself. *Cry out to Him and watch Him drive away every fear!*

PRAYER

Lord, I thank You for Your amazing love. I thank You for saving me and for making me Your child. I thank You that You jealously protect me from the attacks of the enemy and keep me under the shadow of Your wing. Help me continually to find all my security in You and You alone—not in the things of this world. Let those who do not know You visibly see Your loving care for me, that they, too, might know You as a loving God.

I pray this in name of Jesus!

DECLARATION

I declare that I continually dwell under the shadow of the Almighty God. I will fear no evil because the Lord is always with me, and He is my Protector. No weapon that is formed against me shall prosper, and every design of the enemy against my life will come to nothing—that is my heritage as a believer.

I declare this by faith in Jesus' name!

QUESTIONS

1. In what are you placing your security? Are you putting your trust in your finances, your job, or other earthly things; or are you resting securely under the shadow of the Almighty God?
2. Can you think of a time when the Lord protected you from the onslaught of the enemy?
3. Are you currently going through a situation in which you need the shelter of the Lord's protection? Have you called out to Him for deliverance?

DAY 4

ידע

yada

Direction Comes through Deep Intimacy with God

> Trust in the Lord with all thine heart; and lean not unto
> thine own understanding. In all thy ways acknowledge
> Him, and He shall direct thy paths.
> – Proverbs 3:5-6

One of the biggest moments of the year for millions of football fans is the coin toss at the beginning of the Super Bowl. Sadly, many people approach the major decisions of their life in a manner that is just as random. Do you truly need wisdom? Do you want to know what the will of God is for your life? When you are facing a decision, what is the first thing that you are likely to do? Do you create a list of pros and cons? Do you ask your family or friends; or do you simply flip a coin?

The book of Proverbs, written by King Solomon, is renowned for its wisdom. Before Solomon even begins to delve into his pithy sayings, he devotes the first nine chapters to the pursuit of wisdom. This brings us to a fundamental difference between human wisdom and Godly wisdom. Human wisdom is knowledge which is sought for the sake of knowledge itself, or for some sort of personal gain— whether it may be in one's finances, relationships, or whatever the need may be. By contrast, Godly wisdom is a by-product of being in a covenant relationship with the Lord. This contrast between human wisdom and Godly wisdom is highlighted in Proverbs 3:5-6.

As the Lord had commanded the children of Israel to seek Him with all their heart in Deuteronomy 6:4-5, so Solomon gives the same counsel to his son, to whom the book of Proverbs is addressed. In the same way, we exhorted are to lean not on our own understanding. This is not to say that we must not use our God-given mind to guide us; but rather, that we are to seek first the mind and will of God in our daily lives.

When I was in high school, I dislocated my kneecap and had to walk on crutches for six weeks. In addition to the hassle of climbing stairs and juggling books, I had to walk between two campus buildings which were separated by a large football field. Those who have walked on crutches can relate to the sore upper arms and armpits and to the limits that crutches can put on the mobility which we so often take for granted. Likewise, to lean on our own understanding alone carries the same idea in the spiritual realm, in that we are limiting ourselves to our own abilities and resources instead of tapping into the unlimited power of God.

We now come to the crux of this passage. The King James translation of the word "acknowledge" is deceptively bland because it simply gives the idea of simply checking in with God to make sure we are on the right side of His will. In reality, the original Hebrew text carries a much richer meaning. The root word from which "acknowledge" is *yada*. *Yada* means "to know." This is not simply a knowing in the mind, but a knowing in the heart which springs from a deep, personal relationship with God. This word is so intimate that it is often used in several places in the Old Testament in reference to sexual intercourse (Genesis 4:1, Genesis 4:17, Genesis 4:25; Genesis 24:16; Genesis 38:26; Judges 19:25; 1 Samuel 1:19; 1 Kings 1:4).[13]

The wisdom of God is unfolded to us as we intentionally and passionately seek the Giver of wisdom more than the wisdom itself. Such wonderful revelation comes out of an ongoing, living, vibrant, intimate relationship with God. As we cultivate that relationship and spend time seeking His face, God's will for our lives will become crystal clear; and as the Scripture promises, He will direct our paths. *Do you desire to know the will of God? Spend time soaking in His wonderful presence, and you will be utterly amazed at how He will reveal His endless love to you!*

PRAYER

Lord, I love You with all my heart. I am in awe that You would want to know me! Such love from the Creator of the universe is too amazing for me to fathom! I thank You that You have called me out of darkness and into Your marvelous light, not simply for the sake of saving me from hell, but because You desire to have an intimate relationship with me. Lord, I thank You that You are continually drawing me into Your presence by the wooing and drawing of Your Holy Spirit. I thank You that my times of prayer and fellowship go beyond my simply making petitions, but that You speak mysteries to me and You lead me and guide me into greater and greater realms of Your glory!

I pray this in name of Jesus!

DECLARATION

I declare that my hunger for the Lord is insatiable!. Nothing short of knowing Him intimately will satisfy me. As I spend time with Him, I am able to hear Him clearly and to discern His voice as He speaks mysteries to me. I am rooted and grounded in my relationship with the Lord, and it is out of that relationship that I am led by the Shepherd of my soul.

I declare this by faith in Jesus' name!

QUESTIONS

1. In what areas of your life do you need the wisdom of God?
2. Are you only seeking the Lord for His direction for your personal benefit or because you love Him and simply want to spend time with Him?
3. Even if the Lord never spoke to you in your prayer time, would you still love Him?

DAY 5

צנה

tsinnah

The Lord Surrounds Us with His Protective Favor

For thou, Lord, wilt bless the righteous; with favor wilt
thou compass him as with a shield.
– Psalm 5:12

Are you under attack from your enemies? Is your security being threatened? Are you being slandered? Are you under spiritual attack from an unseen enemy through such things as sickness or tormenting thoughts? King David knew firsthand what it was to have vicious enemies. After all, he spent the early years of his reign on the run from King Saul, who out of jealousy tried to kill him on numerous occasions. Later in his reign, David had to flee for his life from Jerusalem when his own son Absalom led a coup to overthrow him. Many of the Psalms came out of moments in David's life when he had nowhere to turn but the Lord for deliverance.

Psalm 5 is one of those desperate prayers from the heart; yet in spite of the anguished tone, David ends the Psalm on a positive note with a reminder to himself of the Lord's faithfulness to protect those who put their trust in Him. *For thou, Lord, wilt bless the righteous; with favor wilt thou compass him as with a shield.* In other passages of the Bible, God's blessing and favor often speak of financial prosperity, but in the context of Psalm 5, His blessing and favor refer specifically to His divine protection.

The Hebrew word for the shield described in this verse is *tsinnah*, which specifically refers to a large shield which is able to cover the entire body.[14] Human shields, however large they may be, do have one fatal weakness—they can only protect one side of the body at a time. They may cover the front part of the body, but if the enemy wants to launch a simultaneous attack from another direction from the rear, there is a side which remains exposed. To use a modern example, our computers may have a good firewall to protect against malicious viruses, but hackers always seem to be able to find their way in through a back door.

The Lord's protection is not so! Psalm 5:12 promises that the Lord not only blocks us from the attacks of the enemy, but He completely surrounds us and leaves no exposed side. The Hebrew verb for surround, *atar*,[15] (translated "compass" in the King James Version) is a rare word, found in only one other verse in the Old Testament—1 Samuel 23:26, when King David is completely surrounded by King Saul's army.[16] David is miraculously delivered from Saul's army only after a messenger comes to King Saul and announces that the Philistines have invaded the land of Israel, causing Saul to withdraw his army to fight the invasion. In Psalm 5:12, David confidently declares that he is encompassed not by the enemy, but by the Lord's protection. It is worth noting that the same root verb *atar* is used in the noun *atarah*,[17] which means a crown or a wreath. Like the crown of thorns which was weaved and put upon the head of Jesus by the Roman soldiers, so the Lord weaves a hedge of protection all around those who love Him.

While on the subject of thorns, it is interesting to note that the Hebrew word for shield, *tsinnah*, which we have already discussed, is furthermore rooted in the word *tsen*, which means "thorn" or "barb." This is a word which is found in the original Hebrew text of Proverbs 22:5 and Job 5:5 with reference to thorns.[18] Indeed, in addition to referring to a large shield, *tsinnah* in some contexts may also refer to a hook or a barb, like that used in a fishing spear (see Amos 4:2).[19]

The wilderness of Zin, through which the Israelites wandered after the Exodus for forty years, is likewise a transliteration of the Hebrew word *tsin*[20] which is rooted in the same word as *tsen*; hence, "Zin" describes the thorns which were a prominent feature of that inhospitable desert. Have you ever noticed how small prey like rabbits and birds like to run to the cover of thorn bushes when approached by people or wild predators? They instinctively know that they are safe under the cover of a thorny hedge of protection. Our human adaptation to protect our perimeters has become barbed or razor wire fences. So it is with the child of God—though we may be weak and defenseless in our own natural strength and resources, we can always run under the cover of our Almighty God and find refuge under His protection.

Sometimes it seems as if our lives are spinning hopelessly out of control. We find ourselves feverishly doing all we can just to put out fires in our lives, having no idea where the next one might break out. Thankfully, we are not alone in this life. The Lord is always near if we will simply call upon His name to help and deliver us. *Are you overwhelmed today? Surrender your problems to the Lord and rest in His complete, divine protection which only He can provide. Stand and see His glorious deliverance!*

PRAYER

Lord Jesus, I am tired of fighting my own battles. You know that I have vicious enemies, both seen and unseen, and I feel powerless to defend myself in my own strength. Thank You for the protection which You, as my Lord and my King, have promised to those who love You. I thank You that Your protection is complete and impenetrable. I give my life to You today, with all of its problems and difficulties, and I trust in You to faithfully protect me from the schemes and wiles of the enemy. Thank You that You empower me to overcome every attack in my life, through the power of Your Holy Spirit who lives in me.

I pray this in name of Jesus!

DECLARATION

I declare that the Lord is my God, my King, and my Protector. I confess that He surrounds my life with a hedge of protection, and that the enemy cannot destroy me. No weapon that is formed against me shall prosper—this is my heritage as a child of the King. I rest in the confidence of knowing that, regardless of what I may see with my natural eyes, the Lord is watching over me, and that even when it seems like I am outnumbered and outgunned by the enemy, the Lord causes me to triumph in every situation in my life.

I declare this by faith in Jesus' name!

QUESTIONS

1. What trials are you facing in your life today?
2. What does the Word of God declare about your situation?
3. In what ways has the Lord delivered you in the past when you had nowhere else to turn but Him?

DAY 6

הגה

hagah

A Personal Invitation to Biblical Meditation

> This book of the law shall not depart out of thy mouth; but thou shalt meditate therein day and night, that thou mayest observe to do all that is written therein: for then thou shalt make thy way prosperous, and then thou shalt have good success.
> – Joshua 1:8

When you hear the word "meditation," what image does it conjure up in your mind? Yoga? Chanting mantras in a lotus position? The Hebrew concept of meditation has a specific meaning which is quite different than what we are normally led to understand. As we learn to enter into biblical meditation, it can greatly benefit our spiritual growth, as well as yield wonderful promises for our lives.

First, we begin with a little background to set the scene. At the outset of Joshua 1, Moses has just died in the wilderness and Joshua has been chosen by the Lord to be his successor to lead the Israelites into the Promised Land. Joshua feels overwhelmed at such a responsibility, so the Lord is not only encouraging, but commanding him, to be strong and courageous and to trust in His power and presence.

The Lord exhorts Joshua that the book of the law is not to depart out of his mouth. John Calvin, in his commentary of the book of Joshua, asked the question, "But why does He forbid him to allow the Law to depart from his mouth rather than from his eyes?" In our day and age, we live in a private culture where it is considered more socially acceptable to read and study the Bible silently on our own instead of openly sharing it with others; Calvin's interpretation of Joshua 1:8, however, was that the law was not intended to be for Joshua's benefit only, but that he in turn was to teach the Word to the people of God.[21] So it is with us…it is not God's optimal intent that we be a dammed-up reservoir of truth, hoarding God's Word to ourselves, but rather, that we might be a free-flowing conduit of God's Word to our family, our friends, our brothers and sisters in Christ, and especially to those who do not know Him. To use a common illustration, the Dead Sea in Israel is stagnant because it has no outlet. Stagnancy is odorous and breeds slime and mosquitoes. The otherwise life-giving water flowing down the Jordan from the springs in the north of Israel simply dumps into the Dead Sea and has nowhere else to go.

Joshua 1:8 continues, "But thou shalt meditate therein day and night." What does it really mean to meditate on the Word of God? The Hebrew word is *hagah*, which can also be translated, "to moan, growl, utter, speak, or muse."[22] Biblical meditation is not just a silent, inward, mental exercise—it inherently involves verbally speaking. Think of how, when we really want to remember something, we like to repeat it aloud, perhaps several times. When I was in seminary, I would study for exams by walking around my tiny apartment and reading or repeating the information aloud, over and over again. If I want to remember something, it is not enough for me to think about it silently in my mind—I must hear myself saying it loudly into my own ears.

Several years ago, I had the amazing privilege of visiting the Holy Land. One morning, I gained a beautiful picture of biblical meditation when I went down to the hotel lobby and encountered several elderly Jewish gentlemen who made it their daily practice to read the Hebrew Scriptures aloud. Contrary to our Western culture in which few men would dare to be so unabashedly public in their devotions, these gentlemen did not seem to be at all distracted by my presence. The presence of the Lord was so real to them that it was as if they were chatting with an old friend over breakfast. This is the simple intimacy which brings delight to the Lord.

Joshua 1:8 concludes with a dual promise, both to Joshua and to those who meditate today on the Word of God daily. The King James Version states, "For then thou shalt make thy way prosperous, and then thou shalt have good success." While in the English translation, these two promises may sound redundant, it is always important to remember that the Lord does not waste words. This is not a redundancy, but a reference to two distinct sources of success.

The first source of success is that which comes through the supernatural blessing of being in relationship with the Lord. In the promise, "Thou shalt make thy way prosperous," the Hebrew verb for prosper is *tsalach*.[23] When we are in covenant with the Lord, His indwelling grace will empower us to be successful in that which we set out to do in His name. The same word is used in 2 Chronicles 31:21, which clearly ties the success of King Hezekiah to his relationship with God, and his faithfulness to follow His commandments.[24] In our fallen humanity, we often excuse sin by compartmentalizing our lives and the lives of others. We say, for example, that one's moral character has no effect on his or her ability to be a leader. In the Kingdom of God, however, nothing could be further from the truth! Proverbs 28:13 declares, "He that covereth his sins shall not prosper: but whoso confesseth and forsaketh them shall have mercy."

The second source of success is that which results from walking in natural wisdom. "Thou shalt have good success," is rooted in the Hebrew verb *sakal*, which refers to the benefits which are available to all people by virtue of using natural wisdom. One theological dictionary describes *sakal* as "a successful life characterized by blessings and well-being in the more comprehensive sense of the sort bestowed upon the wise person according to wisdom instruction."[25] There are natural laws which bring natural consequences to people, regardless of their relationship to God. If those laws are obeyed, they will bring rewards; but if they are violated, they will bring destruction.

If walking in wisdom brings positive results, then why are so many people seemingly bent on making poor choices? The answer to this question is clear. The world system under the sway of the evil one bombards people daily with multiple lies that defy God's Word, through every form of media, including television, movies, books, newspapers, and every other form of popular entertainment and mass communication. Think about it...how many times each day do television programs encourage and glorify sexual promiscuity without mentioning any of its negative consequences? It is a fulfillment of what the prophet Isaiah lamented when he wrote, "Woe unto them that call evil good, and good evil; that put darkness for light, and light for darkness; that put bitter for sweet, and sweet for bitter" (Isaiah 5:20). The only antidote to discern truth and light in a world of lies and darkness is by meditating on the Word of God daily. *Do you want to experience success in your life? Don't just make biblical meditation a stale practice. Ask the Lord to make it your consuming passion!*

PRAYER

Lord, I thank You that You have revealed the truth of Your Word to me. I thank You that Your Holy Spirit within me has infused a passion to know Your Word—not just in my head, but deep down in my heart. I thank You that the more I meditate on Your Word, the more You reveal Your truth to me and empower me to experience victory in my life and success in everything that I do.

I pray this in name of Jesus!

DECLARATION

I declare that my mind is being renewed daily as I meditate on the Word of God. I hide the Word of God in my heart, so I will not sin against the Lord. I am a child of the King through the blood covenant which He made with me through the death and resurrection of His Son Jesus Christ. Because of this covenant, I am blessed in every area of my life. He does not just help me survive each day—He gives me overwhelming, overcoming victory and success!

I declare this by faith in Jesus' name!

QUESTIONS

1. Is biblical meditation a dutiful duty or a passionate passion to you?
2. When was a time in your life that you experienced success as a direct result of your being in intimate relationship with the Lord?
3. What is an area in your life in which you need to see the Lord's victory today? What scriptural truth are you declaring over that situation?

DAY 7

קוֹל

qol

The Voice of the Lord Is Like Thunder

> The voice of the Lord is upon the waters: the God of
> glory thundereth: the Lord is upon many waters.
> – Psalm 29:3

When I was young, my grandparents once hosted a large family reunion at their home in northern Minnesota. During the evening an electrical storm rolled in and turned an otherwise uneventful night into an unforgettable, jarring experience. There was a sudden, ear-splitting crash of thunder, followed by a statically-charged blue haze in the air which seemed to make time stand still for several seconds. Then, as suddenly as it appeared, the haze instantly vanished, leaving everyone staring dumbfounded at each other for several seconds, too terrified to move. The storm rolled on and the next morning we found that a bolt of lightning had corkscrewed around a tall pine tree in the yard next door.

The Lord, in His mercy, has chosen to veil the fullness of His majesty to humanity in this earthly life. There is coming a day, however, when every person will see with their own eyes the glory of God. From time to time throughout the Bible, the Lord likes to pull back the veil to provide momentary glimpses of His glory, as that which is described in Psalm 29. When one reads of the power of God described in this psalm, one cannot help but be overwhelmed by His unspeakable majesty. The writer, King David, declares, "The voice of the Lord is upon the waters." The Hebrew word for voice, is *qol*.

While *qol* normally means "voice," "noise" or "sound," it can also be translated to literally mean a "thunder clap or peal."[26] This word alone is found no less than seven times in Psalm 29. David goes on to write, "The God of glory thundereth." The Hebrew verb for thunder is *ra'am*.[27] This verb is onomatopoeic.[28] As an exercise, say the word "*ra'am*" aloud…Does this word not sound exactly like a bolt of lightning? This psalm describes the Lord's voice alone! In the nineteenth century, the great preacher Charles Spurgeon marveled, "If his voice be thus mighty, what must his hand be!"[29]

When I read about the "waters" in this verse, I am reminded of visiting Niagara Falls as a child. On the United States' side of the falls, the water tumbles over a one hundred seventy-six foot cliff at a staggering rate of one hundred fifty thousands gallons per second. Over the other falls on the Canadian side, the water crashes over at a rate of six hundred thousands gallons per second. The sound of this mighty torrent is awe-inspiring and almost deafening! In the specific context of Psalm 29:3, commentators seem to be split over what is meant by "waters." Some interpret the waters to refer to the sea, while others believe it refers to the sky (see Genesis 1:7). Either way, the original Jewish audience would have recognized this as an allusion to pagan gods who were worshipped by the surrounding Canaanites. The chief Canaanite god most frequently mentioned in the Old Testament is Baal, the god of thunder, lightning, and storms. Archeologists have found numerous idols and images of Baal holding lightning in his hand, not only representing his power over nature, but his power for victory in battle. In addition, the Canaanites worshipped Yam, who was a chaotic god who stirred up the sea. According to mythology, Yam had been conquered by Baal. Psalm 29:3 is a declaration of the Lord's supremacy over both gods.[30] Ultimately, He is the supreme Lord over all gods.

We live in a fallen world which is in a state of rebellion against the Almighty God. At every turn, He is blasphemed and His very existence is shut out of the public square. In such an environment of hostility against the Creator, it is easy to become discouraged and to wonder where God is. Psalm 29 is a reminder of the magnificent glory and the unspeakable, awe-inspiring majesty of His throne. This psalm is a call to worship Him. When we remember who He really is and think on the fullness of His glory, we cannot help but fall prostrate before Him in praise and adoration.

What are you facing today? Are you overwhelmed by the circumstances of life? Are you being slandered or assaulted by your enemies? Remember that there is a God who loves you more than you will ever know. He is not powerless. On the contrary, He is the source of all power and strength in the entire universe. He made it all, and He holds it all together by His very word. *Give your life to Him and entrust your greatest needs to Him, and watch Him show His mighty power on your behalf.*

PRAYER

Lord, I thank You that You are God and that you are my God. I praise You because You are Almighty and All-Powerful. Although You hold all power in the universe, You lovingly choose to restrain that power which could so easily destroy the world with just one word of Your mouth. Help me to remember the fullness of who You are. As I think about Your omnipotent power, I will praise You and I will proclaim Your name to others.

I pray this in name of Jesus!

DECLARATION

I declare that the Lord is God and He is my God. He is the Supreme God over all. There is no other god beside Him nor is there any god who can even approach Him. I choose to meditate on His power. I choose to worship Him from the depths of my being—not for what He does for me, but because of who He is. He is the King of Kings, the Lord of Lords, and the God of Gods, and I will proclaim His power and glory to others. When I am down, I will remember who He is and I will confidently rest in His power to grant me His victory in every area of my life.

I declare this by faith in Jesus' name!

QUESTIONS

1. How did the Lord speak to you through the devotion today?
2. What storms are you facing in your life today? Are you trusting in His power to deliver you?
3. When you think about the majesty of the Lord, how do you respond? Do you have a deeper desire to worship Him, or do you find yourself intimidated by His awesome power?

DAY 8

כבד

kabed

Blessing Our Parents with Heavy Honor

Honour thy father and thy mother: that thy days may be long
upon the land which the Lord thy God giveth thee.
– Exodus 20:12

I hate you! How many times in the media have we witnessed rebellious children screaming these words defiantly at their parents? How many times have we seen stereotypical images of parents who are depicted as being dumber than their kids? How many times on daytime talk shows have we seen adults complaining about the shortcomings of their mother and father, blaming their own problems and shortcomings on their upbringing? Two thousand years ago, the Apostle Paul warned that in the last days, one of the characteristics of people would be that they would be disobedient to their parents (2 Timothy 3:2). As we look around, we see this prophecy being exponentially fulfilled daily before our very eyes.

This sort of rebellion, however, runs completely counter to God's ideal for society. When the Law was given on Mount Sinai, the Lord was adamant that His own covenant children, the nation of Israel, were to have no part in this rebellious spirit. So important was this to God, that He included the command to honor father and mother in the Ten Commandments (Exodus 20:12).

The very first word in Exodus 20:12, "Honor" is translated from the Hebrew verb *kabed*, which means, "to be heavy, weighty, honoured."[31] Even in the English language, we describe serious matters as being heavy, while describing frivolous matters as being light. The honor which God commands toward father and mother cannot be overstated. One commentator observes that this honor goes beyond a simple attitude of the heart—it must also be expressed in our words and in our actions.[32]

In addition, this honor is not to be limited solely to our biological parents. It is also intended to be extended to other authority figures in our lives, including teachers, spiritual leaders, and even government leaders.[33] We see an example of this in 2 Kings 2:12, when the prophet Elisha cries out "My father! My father!" when his mentor, the prophet Elijah, is taken up into heaven.[34]

Several years ago, I was chatting with a friend of mine in Mexico. After I told her that I lived in a different region than my mother and father and sisters, she suddenly had a horrified look on her face. When I asked her what was wrong, she looked at me with wide-eyed wonder and asked me if I hated my family! Of course I did not; but in Latin American culture, it is generally unthinkable for a family member to move far away from his or her relatives.

The commandment to honor our parents is unconditional. Even if we do not condone their behavior, we are nonetheless expected to give them the honor which the Lord commands. One commentator writes, "Woe to the father whose cruelty, selfishness, or evil passions make it hard for his child to understand the Archetype, because the type is spoiled…But how much sorer woe to the son who dishonors his earthly parent, and in so doing slays within himself the very principle of obedience to the Father of Spirits!"[35]

This is a commandment which comes with a promise. The Lord promised that the Israelites' days would be long in the land which He was giving to them. If the children were to stop honoring their parents, there was a very real danger that they would consequently reject the God of their fathers, and the nation would go into apostasy.

On a personal level, a major benefit of honoring our parents is that Scripture promises that doing so can prolong our individual lives. God has established the authority of the father and mother to instill right and wrong into the hearts of the children. Those children who defy and disparage the authority of their parents are more likely to have destructive lifestyles, consequently living shorter lives due to violence, disease, and a host of other factors. On the other hand, those who honor their parents tend to be better-adjusted and are less likely to fall into destructive lifestyles, thus living longer lives. The blessing of God can supernaturally produce long, fulfilling lives for those who put their trust in Him.

Sometimes we are content with exerting the least amount of effort necessary to maintain our relationships. We may have a feeling of respect toward our parents, but that feeling may never be translated into outward action. We may buy expensive Christmas presents for our parents, but we may never take the time to simply call them to tell them that we love them. True Godly love often requires that we go beyond our normal comfort zone. God the Father gave His Son, Jesus Christ, to die on the cross for our sins, holding nothing back in expressing His love for us. How much more should we be willing to lay down our time, our emotions, our pride, or whatever the Lord may ask of us, that we might be vessels of His love toward those who brought us into the world? *Who is the Lord laying upon your heart right now to bless through your words or life or acts of kindness towards them? Why not reach out to them right now and touch them with the love of God? Who knows what amazing, unexpected things that God will do in that relationship?*

PRAYER

Lord Jesus, I thank You for my mother and father. Thank You for all that they have sacrificed for me. Show me how I can uniquely express my love and gratitude for them, and help me to boldly follow through on what you show me to do. Help me to sincerely honor them—not only in my inner heart, but also in my words and in my actions. Help me to be a vessel of Your love to them.

I pray this in name of Jesus!

DECLARATION

I declare that I am faithful to my mother and father whom You have given to me. I choose to honor them through my attitudes, through my words, and through my actions. I choose to not only honor my natural mother and father, but all of those whom the Lord has placed in authority over me. I will not speak evil of them; but rather, I will faithfully pray for them and speak words of life to and about them.

I declare this by faith in Jesus' name!

QUESTIONS

1. What is the greatest expression of honor that you have ever given to your parents? How might you top that?
2. Who else has the Lord placed in your life to honor the honorable? Have you expressed or shown your gratitude to them lately?
3. What are some specific ways that you might bless those whom the Lord has put upon your heart to honor?

DAY 9

קֹדֶשׁ

qadesh

God's Free Gift to You Is His Holy Nature

And ye shall be holy unto me: for I the Lord am holy, and have severed you from other people, that ye should be mine.
– Leviticus 20:26

Holy mackerel! The word "holy" has so become a part of our daily vernacular that it has been all but stripped of its original reverence. Sadly, this word has even been commonly used as an expletive. Perhaps today as we look at this word in one of its earliest biblical settings, we might not only gain a renewed understanding of what it truly means, but we might be amazingly blessed to realize that it is this very holiness that the Lord freely gives to those who simply trust in Him.

The original Hebrew word for holy which is found in Leviticus 20:26 is *qadesh* (spelled *kadesh* in many English Bible translations). It is synonymous with that which is sacred, or with being "separate from human infirmity, impurity and sin."[36] Most people have a distorted sense of what holiness really is. The average person tends to define holiness strictly by what one does *not* do. There is an old-fashioned expression in religious circles which goes something like this: "I don't smoke; I don't chew; and I don't hang around with people who do." In reality, this is only a partial, legalistic and even distorted definition of what holiness is. In fact, those of us who have known Christ for many years can testify that some of the meanest people in the body of Christ fit this description.

Holiness is not only demonstrated by what one *does not* do, but encompasses the positive attributes of what one *does* do. Ultimately however, true holiness is not defined by but one's *actions*, but by one's *identity*. This holiness cannot be attained by trying to reform or improve ourselves by means of human willpower, but is imparted to us as a gift when we come to a living faith in the Lord Jesus Christ. Rather than trying to generate holiness, we can simply walk out the holiness which is already in us. The source of this goodness can only come from God. A person who is truly holy is one who continually bubbles over with the fruit of the Spirit, as listed in Galatians 5:22-23: "But the fruit of the Spirit is love, joy, peace, longsuffering, gentleness, goodness, faith, meekness, temperance: against such there is no law." Holy people gush with overflowing love towards God and towards others. Holy people speak words of life and encouragement. Holy people have abundant compassion, not only toward loved ones, but to everyone they encounter in their daily lives. Holy people will even travel out of their way to be a blessing to others.

In Leviticus 20, the Lord is addressing the nation of Israel, with whom He is establishing His covenant before they enter into the Promised Land. He is reminding His children the Israelites that He has set them apart unto Himself as a holy people. The verb rendered "set apart" is translated from the Hebrew verb *badal*, which also means, "divided" or "separated."[37] The same verb is used in several other places in the Old Testament: It is used when God divides the waters in Genesis 1:6; it is used when He divides darkness and light, night and day in Genesis 1:14; and it is used with reference to the veil of the temple which divided the Holy Place from the Most Holy Place, in Exodus 26:33.[38] As He did with the Hebrews under the Old Covenant, the Lord has separated New Covenant believers out of the world and unto Himself through faith in the Lord Jesus Christ alone. The first letter of Peter proclaims, "But you are a chosen generation, a royal priesthood, a holy nation, a peculiar people: that you should show forth the praises of Him who hath called you out of darkness into His marvelous light" (1 Peter 2:9).

The holiness of God is a two-edged sword. On the one hand it is separation from the world, demonstrated under the Old Covenant by Israel's prohibition from eating unclean foods which the surrounding nations ate (Leviticus 20:23-25).[39] At the same time, it is separation unto God (Leviticus 20:26).[40] By our own strength, we may manage to separate ourselves to a very limited extent from the world, but only God can separate us unto Him. There is no substitute for the authentic holiness that comes from Him alone.

When I think about true holiness and false holiness, I am reminded of fast food restaurants where the fountain drinks are virtually guaranteed to be watered down, producing a flat taste. Human-based holiness, mixing human effort with Godly fruit, produces the same kind of result in people. Only holiness which comes from God alone is pure and undiluted. We cannot produce authentic holiness by our own willpower. The more we try to do so, the more frustrated we become and the end result ends up being nothing more than self-righteousness and hypocrisy. The glorious news is that the Lord Jesus Christ freely gives us His holiness when we enter into a relationship with Him by faith, putting our whole trust in Him and the salvation which He purchased for us when He went to the cross. Godly holiness is a gift which can only be received and walked out daily by faith. As the expression goes, "Accept no imitations!" *Are you walking in authentic Godly holiness, or are you settling for a cheap counterfeit? Ask the Lord daily to flood you with His holiness, and be amazed as He thoroughly transforms you supernaturally from the inside out.*

PRAYER

Lord Jesus, I thank you that it pleased You to draw me unto Yourself, even when I was still in a state of enmity against You. I acknowledge that by my own strength there is nothing good in me. All that I am is a result of Your loving grace in my life. Please open my eyes to reveal who I am in You and help me always to live up to who You created me to be. Please continue to separate me from the world, and to separate me unto You. Let Your holiness flow through me to others, fueled not by my own smug self-righteousness, but fueled by Your passionate love.

I pray this in name of Jesus!

DECLARATION

I declare that I have been called out of darkness and into the marvelous light of the Kingdom of God. I no longer desire the temporal things of the world. Instead, I passionately desire the eternal things of God. I no longer see myself as a lost sinner, but I see myself as a redeemed saint of God and I live up to what the Lord has called me to be. I am separated from the world and holy unto God, and I live every moment of every day in that reality. God hates sin, so I hate sin. God loves people, so I love people. I reflect the holiness of God in all that I think, in all that I say, and in all that I do. I am a saint of God!

I declare this by faith in Jesus' name!

QUESTIONS

1. What are some examples of human-generated holiness which you have witnessed or experienced? What are some examples of Godly holiness which you have witnessed or experienced?
2. Do you see yourself as holy? Where does your holiness come from?
3. In what ways have you allowed the holy things of God to be mixed with the profane (common) things of this world in your own life? What kind of fruit has this produced in your life?

DAY 10

שָׁקֵד

shaqed

Almond Joy

> And it came to pass, that on the morrow Moses went into the tabernacle of witness; and, behold, the rod of Aaron for the house of Levi was budded, and brought forth buds, and bloomed blossoms, and yielded almonds.
> – Numbers 17:8

What is your favorite candy? During my childhood, I used to love Almond Joy candy bars. In today's devotional, we will learn of the special significance of the almond, and we will see how this nut speaks so beautifully to us of the resurrection of the Lord Jesus Christ.

The original context of today's verse occurs on the heels of a rebellion against the leadership of Moses and Aaron, which occurred during the Israelites' forty years of wilderness wanderings (Numbers 16-17). The anger of the Lord was so fierce that He sent a plague among the people, which claimed 14,700 lives before it was stopped as a result of the intercession of Aaron (Numbers 16:46-49). Immediately after the dust had settled, the Lord commanded each of the tribes to bring a staff to the tabernacle, with the name of the tribal leader written upon each respective rod. Some commentators believe that Aaron's staff was in addition to the twelve tribal staffs, which would make a total of thirteen staffs.[41] Regardless of whether there were twelve or thirteen staffs, the one staff that would bloom would reveal the Lord's chosen leader. At the outset of this test, Aaron's staff, like the rest, had no more life in it than a dead stick; yet the very next day, it was discovered that his staff alone had budded and bloomed with blossoms and almonds.

Here, our focus will be upon the symbolism of the almond. In Numbers 17:8, the Hebrew word for almond is *shaqed*.[42] To this day in Israel the almond is the plant first to be harvested in the calendar year, in late January or early February.[43] The Hebrew noun *shaqed* (almond) is, in fact, formed from the participle form of the verb *shaqad,* which means, "to wake" or "to watch." Literally, *shaqed* could be translated as "the waking or watching one," as one who mourns at a funeral vigil.[44] Likewise, almonds are pictured as keeping watch over the wintry death of creation.

Two thousand years ago, while the whole world was dead in sin and depravity, the Lord Jesus Christ, the Son of God, after He suffered a horrible death on the cross and all seemed lost, rose victoriously from the grave. Colossians 1:18 declares, "And He is the head of the body, the church, who is the beginning, the first-born from the dead; that in all things He might have the pre-eminence." Like the glorious almond blossom that blooms in the dead of winter, Jesus' resurrection heralded the beginning of a newly redeemed creation. He alone offers us the promise of a brand new life—a resurrection from the ash heap of our own destruction. *Have you experienced the power of Christ's resurrection in your life? Regardless of how hopeless your current circumstances may seem, He stands ready today to bring complete restoration to your broken life...All you need to do is ask!*

PRAYER

Lord Jesus, I thank You that You are my God. You hold the power of life and death in Your hands because You are the source of all life. I thank You that, even if it seems like there is nothing but death and destruction in my life, there is nothing which is too far gone for You to bring restoration. I bring the broken pieces of my life to You today, and I ask that You breathe Your resurrection power into my life to create something beautiful so that You may be glorified for all to see.

I pray this in name of Jesus!

DECLARATION

I declare that the Lord Jesus Christ has risen from the dead. By His death and resurrection, I, too, have been raised up in newness of life with Him. There is nothing that is impossible to those who believe. The Lord Jesus Christ breathes His resurrection power into every area of death in my life, and He makes everything new. I make myself available today to be a vessel through which His resurrection power might flow to others. Where there is despair, I will bring His hope; and where there is death, I will bring His life.

I declare this by faith in Jesus' name!

QUESTIONS

1. What are some other biblical accounts that you can recall which demonstrate the Lord's resurrection power?
2. What are some miracles of that the Lord has done in your life?
3. Are there any areas of death in your life today which need the power of Christ's resurrection? Do you believe in your heart that He can bring restoration to those circumstances?

DAY 11

יָצַר

yatsar

You Have Been Personally Handmade by God

> And the Lord God formed man of the dust of the
> ground, and breathed into his nostrils the breath of life;
> and man became a living soul.
> – Genesis 2:7

We live in a world in which the vast majority of the products we use daily are mass-produced, from automobiles to dental floss. I once saw a television program which even showed the process of mass-production of baby chicks! Unfortunately, we have in some ways come to view people as being mass-produced, as well. I have been no less guilty of such calloused thought patterns; in fact, I have frequently described myself in high school as being "part of the faceless masses." In a "Made-in-China" kind of world, handmade items have become a precious commodity and are hence intrinsically more valuable. Because of their superior quality, handmade products command a higher price—whether they might be European sports cars or Amish wood furniture.

Everyday, we are inundated with images of murder victims in the news and entertainment media. The result has been that we have been desensitized to the intrinsic, priceless value of human life to such an extent that the tragedy of human death has been reduced to little more than a statistic. How far we have fallen from recognizing the crowning jewel of creation which God made us to be! The natural result of the dogmatic teaching of evolution, so atheistic in nature and so prevalent in our Western culture, has been the conclusion by many that human life is devoid of meaning and purpose…And why not? After all, if we are only the product of a series of random evolutionary processes, how can we believe anything more?

The reality is that nothing could be further from the truth! Genesis 2:7 reflects the tender affection with which God created Adam, the first human being. The care with which He created Adam provides a glimpse of His love for all humanity who would follow. In this verse, the word "formed" comes from the Hebrew word *yatsar,* which is used in the Old Testament with reference to a potter forming a pot of clay (See also Isaiah 29:16; Jeremiah 18:4-6).[45] God formed Adam from the dust of the earth. While in our mind's eye we may picture a clod of dirt, the word for "dust," *aphar,* is more likened to a very fine powder.[46] Imagine what incredible perseverance it would take to create something as complex as a human being, working with nothing more than microscopic particles!

In spite of all the time and energy that God had poured into forming Adam, he still remained a lifeless form. It was not until God breathed into Adam that he "became a living soul." When God breathed into Adam, He was not merely blowing oxygen into his lungs; rather, God was breathing the essence of his very life into His new, beloved creation. No other creature in all of creation has been given such a marvelous privilege of being infused with the very life of God Himself!

Genesis 2:7 concludes, "And man became a living soul." In the entertainment media, the soul is grossly misrepresented in a myriad of ways. Children's cartoons tend to illustrate the soul as an imaginary heart. Movies depict the soul as something which can be bought and sold. The Jewish concept of the soul, however, is quite different from the well-known stereotypes of Western culture.

The Hebrew word for soul is *nephesh,* a comprehensive word which, depending on the context can also be translated in any of the following ways: "living being, life, self, person, desire, appetite, emotion, and passion."[47] Our Western understanding of the three-part being of spirit, soul, and body was formulated by the Greeks. The spirit is the highest part of us which communes with God; the soul comprises of our mind, will, and emotions; and our body is the physical part of us, in which the invisible spirit and soul dwells.

Contrary to the Greek model, Jewish thinkers have historically favored belief in a two-part being in which the soul and spirit are inseparably melded together and housed in the physical body. The *nephesh*, which includes both the soul and the spirit, forms the core of one's personality. According to one theological dictionary, it is the seat of a person's "drives, appetites, desires, and will."[48] So central to our being is the soul that one writer observed that to say a person *has* a soul reflects a misunderstanding of what the soul is.[49] One does not *have* a soul; but rather, he or she *is* a soul.

Like the potter skillfully forms the clay, God lovingly formed us and He breathed His life into us. Everything that makes us unique has been infused into us by the breath of God Himself. Within each and every one of us are special gifts which God has given to us for His honor and His glory. Are you artistic? God made you that way. Are you athletic? God made you that way. Are you a leader? Are you merciful? Do you become angered when you see injustice? God put these attributes in you. The things that we love, the things which stir us and the things that move us—all of these passions come from God. That being the case, it logically follows that if we despise others or even ourselves, we are not only disparaging His handiwork—we are insulting God Himself!

Why not take time today to thank God for making you and for the gift that He has made you to be, and which He has provided through the loved ones in your life? The next time you may feel tempted to look down upon yourself or others, stop and remember that God lovingly formed every single one of us. *Do you feel less than valued today? Ask the Lord to show you the unique treasure which He has placed in you, and ask Him that you might supernaturally see yourself through His loving eyes!*

PRAYER

Lord Jesus, I thank You that You have formed me just the way I am, and that You have made all the amazing people in my life. Please open my eyes to see the hidden treasures that You have deposited in me, in each of the people in my life and even in those who are strangers. Help me to see all people through the prism of Your loving eyes, and help me to be an encouragement to them to stir up the gifts within them. Help me not to compare myself to others and to be envious of what You have given them, but help me to rejoice in what You have made all of us to be.

I pray this in name of Jesus!

DECLARATION

I declare that I am fearfully and wonderfully made by God. I am not here by random chance, but I have been made in a special way, for a special purpose, to fulfill a specific destiny. I choose to see the good which God has created in others and in myself. I choose to use all that God has given me for His glory, to bring His kingdom down to the earth.

I declare this by faith in Jesus' name!

QUESTIONS

1. What are some of the passions, dreams, and desires that God has placed in you? How do you believe that the Lord wants to use them for His kingdom?
2. Have you taken the time to encourage others in what God has made them to be?
3. Who are some people in your life today whom you might build up by calling out their unique, God-given gifts?

DAY 12

דבק

dabaq

We Are One with Our Spouse and One with Christ

Therefore shall a man leave his father and his mother, and shall
cleave unto his wife: and they shall be one flesh.
– Genesis 2:24

"Marriage is just a piece of paper." How many times have we heard this expression? In recent years, the institution of marriage has come under increasing fire, maligned as being antiquated and no longer relevant nor necessary in the new "progressive" age. God is good and He is incapable of creating anything that is not good. The reality is that marriage is beneficial for all involved—for women, men, children, and the community at large.

The origin of marriage goes back to Adam and Eve in the Garden of Eden. In Genesis 2:23, the Bible narrates how Eve was formed from the rib of Adam. In the very next verse, God declares that a man shall leave his father and mother, and he shall cleave to his wife, and they shall become one flesh (Genesis 2:24). The key word upon which we will focus today is the word "cleave," which is translated from the Hebrew word *dabaq*, which is also rendered "to cling" or "keep close to."[50] While at first glance, the word seems to be synonymous with hugging, it is actually a verb which expresses a powerful bonding; in fact, the same verb is used in Isaiah 41:7 with reference to "soldering" or "welding" an idol.[51] Dr. William McDonald, Associate Professor of Old Testament at Oral Roberts University, compared the union to gluing two sheets of paper together with superglue and then attempting to pull them apart. One cannot separate them without destroying both sheets.[52]

Genesis 2:24 concludes that the man and woman will become one flesh. One commentator observes that there is a miracle, not fully understood by the natural mind, which takes place in marriage, transcending even the physical, emotional, and spiritual connection which takes place through the sexual union which cements the marital bond. That miracle is that the man and woman are so united that they physically become related to one another in flesh and blood, no less so than the kinship which exists between parents and children and brothers and sisters.[53]

While the idea of such a commitment may surpass our full understanding, the same strength of commitment can help provide a tremendous sense of security. What is even more glorious is that the New Testament alludes to the marital relationship to highlight the strength of the covenant relationship between the Lord Jesus Christ and His bride, which is His Church. In Ephesians 5:29-32, the Apostle Paul marvels at this amazing union between God and His people: "For no man ever yet hated his own flesh; but nourisheth and cherisheth it, even as the Lord the church: For we are members of his body, of his flesh, and of his bones. For this cause shall a man leave his father and mother, and shall be joined unto his wife, and they two shall be one flesh. This is a great mystery: but I speak concerning Christ and the church." In the same way that we become one flesh with our earthly spouse in marriage, we as believers in Christ enter by faith into an everlasting union with Him which is no less binding. We literally become one with Christ, and He with us, and the many blessings of earthly marriage described earlier likewise translate into equivalent spiritual benefits which we receive through our marital covenant with Christ.

Do you sometimes find yourself wondering if you are truly saved from sin? Many believers struggle with such vacillating doubts from time to time. These thoughts do not come from God, but from the enemy of our souls, Satan. He is the accuser of the brethren who derives twisted pleasure in heaping false condemnation upon the people of God (Revelation 12:10). The wonderfully liberating truth is that our relationship with the Lord Jesus Christ is not dependent upon our ability to please Him by our good works. He alone initiated the relationship; He alone sustains the relationship; and He alone will complete the work which He began in us. He alone is the Author and the Finisher of our faith (Hebrews 12:2). *Jesus loves you more than you can even begin to fathom! Rest in the security of His everlasting, never-ending faithfulness to you and walk in the freedom of knowing in you heart that He will never, ever leave you nor forsake you! He is yours and you are His forever!*

PRAYER

Lord Jesus, I thank you for Your amazing love which sought me out and brought me into an everlasting covenant relationship with You. I bless You that I am absolutely secure in You because I have been made one with You. I love You passionately with all of my heart and with all of my being. I come to You earnestly desiring sweet, secret intimacy with You. I long to hear of Your love for me. Help me to be a messenger of Your grace, that I might be the revealer and the mediator of Your covenant to others.

I pray this in name of Jesus!

DECLARATION

I declare that I am the bride of Christ. I am one with Him and my everlasting bond with Him is unbreakable and indissoluble. Truly, He will never leave me nor forsake me. I do not listen to the voice of doubt and insecurity from the evil one, but I rest in my eternal security in Him.

I declare this by faith in Jesus' name!

QUESTIONS

1. In what ways has your understanding of the covenant of marriage been distorted because of childhood memories or past experiences? Have you allowed Jesus entry into your heart to heal those disappointments?
2. What does it look like for you to be one flesh with your spouse?
3. Do you see yourself as the beautiful bride of Christ? Do you see Him as your heavenly Groom?

DAY 13

פלא

pala

His Name Is Gloriously Wonderful!

> And the angel of the Lord said unto him, "Why askest thou thus after my name, seeing it is secret?"
> – Judges 13:18

"In our daily conversation, we like to call everything "wonderful." "The cheesecake was wonderful!" "My house is wonderful!" "My spouse is wonderful!" "The movie was wonderful!" This word has become so common in our vocabulary that its original meaning has been lost. Today we will revisit this word as it was used in the Bible and I believe that you will marvel as you discover how it describes the limitless possibilities which are available to us through the power of the Almighty God.

Throughout the Book of Judges, we find the Israelites, having previously taken hold of the Promised Land by the power of God, to now be in a perpetual cycle of backsliding, oppression by their enemies, repentance, and deliverance through Spirit-empowered military heroes whom God would raise up, who were called "judges." The thirteenth chapter of Judges records the birth of Samson to Manoah and his wife, who was barren. The Israelites at this time had been under the oppression of the Philistines for forty years, but the Lord was now going to raise up Samson, who would be born to Manoah and his wife to deliver the entire nation of Israel through supernatural feats of strength.

The inability to have children can be frustrating in any marriage, but it was especially painful in Israelite culture because infertility was perceived to be a direct curse of judgment from God. There can be no doubt that Manoah and his wife had prayed for years, begging God for any son to simply carry on the family name. One can imagine the desperation that dominated their prayers and pleadings. The Lord, however, had so much more than they could have possibly imagined! He was not only going to give them a son, but he was going to give them the honor of being the parents of a national hero who would single-handedly bring freedom to the entire land. So it is with us...too often, we beg for scraps, having no idea how much the Lord really loves us and wants to bless us beyond our wildest dreams!

The Angel of the Lord who came to announce the birth of Samson to Manoah and his wife was not merely a created angelic messenger of God, but He was the Lord Himself. We know this because Judges 13:22 tells us that Manoah was afraid that he was going to die because he had seen God. Initially however, His true identity was not immediately known to Manoah. In Judges 13:17, after the mysterious visitor had promised a son, Manoah asked for the visitor's name in order that he might properly honor Him after the promise had come to pass. In the biblical culture, one's name was very important, carrying no less importance than the person bearing it.[54] In the ancient biblical culture, names intentionally reflected some attribute which the bearer possessed, or declared an attribute of what the bearer was to become; therefore, a person's name declared the very essence of who that person was. For this reason, the names of God revealed throughout the Bible are especially important because they reveal the essence of who He is.

Instead of answering Manoah's question directly, the Lord responded with another question, "Why askest thou thus after my name, seeing it is secret?" The language in the King James Version is somewhat archaic and tends to blur the full impact of what the Lord was rhetorically asking. The word "secret" is better translated "wonderful," as in the New American Standard Bible.[55] It comes from the Hebrew word *peliy*, which can also be rendered "incomprehensible."[56] By simply changing the word "wonderful" to "full of wonder," we draw closer to its true meaning. The verb form, *pala*, means "to be surpassing" or "extraordinary."[57] Interestingly *peliy* and *pala* are linguistically related to the Hebrew verb *palag*, which means "to split" or "divide."[58] The idea is that there is a sharp contrast between two realities in the universe—the finite realm of humanity and the infinite realm of the power of God.[59] The awesome, wonderful works of God come exclusively from that unseen realm which resides on the other side of the dividing line between the natural and supernatural.

Do you need a huge miracle today? Do you need healing? Do you need a financial breakthrough? Do you need supernatural restoration of a relationship that is beyond repair? Let us recall the words of the Apostle Paul as he triumphantly concludes his prayer in Ephesians 3:20, "Now unto Him that is able to do exceedingly abundantly above all that we ask or think, according to the power that worketh in us." *Don't just believe God for the minimum to get you by! Believe Him to do crazy, over-the-top miracles in your life. There is nothing God cannot do!*

PRAYER

Lord Jesus, I thank You that You are my God! I thank You hold everything in the universe together by Your word. I give my biggest need to You today and I fully believe You for Your very best. Be glorified in my life through mighty miracles, signs and wonders in order that others might see Your goodness and wonder-working power.

I pray this in name of Jesus!

DECLARATION

I declare that I walk by faith and not by sight. I am not limited by what I see around me with my natural eyes; but rather, I believe God to do things in my life that my mind cannot even conceive. Nothing is impossible with God! He is my Healer, my Provider and my Deliverer! His name is wonderful!

I declare this by faith in the mighty name of Jesus!

QUESTIONS

1. In light of the devotion today, what do you now think of when you hear the word "wonderful"?
2. What kind of miracle do you need from the Lord today, whether for yourself or a loved one?
3. Do you have a dream in your heart which seems impossible by human standards? Can you believe God to exceed your wildest expectations?

DAY 14

נר

ner

His Word Lights My Path

Thy word is a lamp unto my feet, and a light unto my path.
— Psalm 119:105

Years ago when I was in the United States Air Force, I was deployed to Egypt for six months. The base where I was stationed was remotely located way out in the middle of the desert; as such, there was very little lighting at night. On a moonless night, once you were away from the light of the buildings, the desert would be so dark that you could not see your hand in front of your face.

One late night, after a watching a movie, my roommate and I had to walk through the blackness to get back home. I wanted to take the road back, which, though it would have taken longer, was safer because it was paved and the footing was sure. My roommate, on the other hand, wanted to take a shortcut across the sand, in spite of both of our knowing that there were deep holes everywhere which were invisible at night. After some arguing, we decided to take the shortcut across the sand. No sooner had we walked a couple hundred feet off the road than I stepped into thin air and fell into a pit which was about three to four feet deep. Thankfully I was not hurt, except for my pride!

This anecdote is a perfect illustration of today's verse. Throughout Psalm 119, the psalmist declares his love for the Word of God, of which the revelation up to that time was limited to the Old Testament Law. Psalm 119:105, one of the most well-known and beloved verses in the entire Bible, metaphorically draws out two ways by which God's Word gives light. While on the surface, the verse may seem to possess a poetic redundancy, one must remember that every word in the Bible has a specific meaning and purpose. As we look at this verse, we will see that the two forms of light highlight two respective functions of God's Word.

In the first half of the verse, the light of God's Word is described as a lamp. The Hebrew word used is *ner*,[60] which refers to the portable oil-filled lamps which in biblical times were carried around at night like flashlights would be carried today. Archeologists have unearthed clay lamps which provide a picture of what a *ner* might have looked like. The earliest lamps which have been found were simply shaped like an open shell; while later lamps evolved to have a flat base and a small spout to hold the wick[61] As time progressed, the lamps became more elaborately decorated. In the New Testament, Jesus makes reference to lampstands, which were high pedestals in the home on which lamps were placed in order to provide maximum light (Mark 4:10).[62] By the same token, the Book of Job makes reference to lamps being hung high up under the roof of a tent for the same purpose (Job 18:6; Job 29:3).[63] To this day, it is a Bedouin custom to keep a lamp lit in the tent throughout the night to ward off demons.[64]

The imagery of the lamp reveals how the Word shines the light of God's truth upon sin. The sinful man or woman who does not know God is completely blinded by sin and oblivious to its destruction—not only in his or her own life, but also in the lives of others. God's Word warns us of the dangers of sin; and if we will heed those warnings, we can keep from being bit by its consequences. Going back to the incident of my falling into the hole, if I had been carrying a flashlight, I could have seen the hazard coming and steered clear of it. So it is with the light of God's Word. Through the revelation of the Word of God, we are warned in advance of sin so we can steer clear of its danger.

The nineteenth-century preacher Charles Spurgeon paints a vivid picture of lamp-bearing in biblical times: "Having no fixed lamps in eastern towns, in old time each passenger carried a lantern with him that he might not fall into the open sewer, or stumble over the heaps of ordure which defiled the road."[65] I am reminded of a brief time when I was residing at a campus on the outskirts of Dallas. This particular area was home to many poisonous snakes. The guests were therefore warned to always carry a flashlight when walking outside at night, lest they should inadvertently step on any snakes which might be lying on the road to soak up the warmth left over from the heat of the day.

The second half of Psalm 119:105 goes on to say that the Word of God is "a light unto my path." The Hebrew word for light is *owr*. In contrast to *ner*, which refers to a portable lamp, the word *owr* is often used in the Old Testament in reference to sunlight, daylight, dawn, and even moonlight.[66] References to the lights of the heavens in the creation account (Genesis 1:14-16) utilize the plural form of *or*.[67] While the lamp guides us little by little through the darkness of sin and confusion, the light of day gives us a long range view of God's will for our lives. One author described the difference succinctly, stating, "A light shows us the road; a lamp shows us the next step."[68] While the Bible does not give us specific, play-by-play answers for every single decision with which we are faced, it does provide us with enough of a framework of His will that we will be able to discern God's direction for our lives. To illustrate this, I have lived on the front range of Colorado for over twenty years. Anyone who lives here knows that if one ever gets lost, he or she can always remember that the mountains are west. At night however, the mountains are invisible, making it much easier to get lost and disoriented after dark.

Do you continually find yourself in one jam after another because you have fallen into messes brought about by poor choices? Do you feel lost, confused, and disoriented when it comes to making decisions in your life? *Trust and abide in the Word of God to light your way! The Holy Spirit will never lead you astray!*

PRAYER

Lord Jesus, I thank You that You have not left me to my own devices to blindly grope my way through life; but that You have given me Your Word and You have sent Your Holy Spirit to reside in me, to illuminate the truth of Your Word to me. Thank You that through Your Word, You keep me from falling into the trap of sin and You lead me in Your paths of righteousness. I love Your Word, and I choose to live my life, moment by moment, day by day and year by year, according to Your revealed truth. Please give me an insatiable hunger to hide Your Word in my heart so that I might not sin against You and that I might fulfill all of Your plans and purposes for my life.

I pray this in name of Jesus!

DECLARATION

I declare that I am the light of the world, because the Lord Jesus Christ, the Light of the world, has saved me and has sent His Holy Spirit to light my way. I do not walk in darkness, because He has called me out of darkness and into His marvelous light. I have a passion for God's Word and I walk in the light of God's Word every day of my life. His Word exposes sin. His Word leads and guides me in His paths of righteousness. I am not confused; but rather, I boldly go forth with the confidence that He is directing my steps to fulfill His good and perfect will.

I declare this by faith in Jesus' name!

QUESTIONS

1. Are there any sinful patterns in your life with which you constantly seem to struggle? What does the Word of God say about those sins; and what does it say about your authority over those sins? Are you exercising your authority by speaking the Word of God to overcome those sins?
2. Do you feel like you are going in the Lord's direction for your life or do you feel like you are wandering around in a wilderness of confusion?
3. Can you think of a time that the Word of God kept you from the snare of sin, or has given you guidance and direction?

DAY 15

ירא

yare

The Desirable Fear of the Lord

The fear of the Lord is the beginning of knowledge:
but fools despise wisdom and instruction.
– Proverbs 1:7

"Some time ago, I was dog-sitting for some friends who had gone on vacation. It was the Fourth of July, and coupled with all the firecrackers that were being lit all over the neighborhood, a thunderstorm had rolled in. These combined factors created the perfect storm of terror for both of the dogs who were under my care. Consequently, they were absolutely terrified from all the loud noises and the lightning to the point that they were violently shaking. When I think of those dogs on that day, I am reminded that many people have the same fear toward God. This paralyzing fear produces a "fight or flight syndrome" which leads some to rebel against God, while driving others away from His presence.

Throughout the Bible, there are many references to the fear of the Lord, but what it actually means to fear God is not clearly defined. One writer observes that in the Bible, fear itself has a wide range of meanings which can only be discerned by studying the context of each respective passage where fear is addressed.[69] In Proverbs 1:7, "the fear of the Lord" is a translation of the Hebrew expression *yirat HaShem*.[70] It is desirable for every human being to have a fear of God; but what that fear looks like is dependent upon one's relationship to, or separation from, God. Those who are separated from God are very wise in fearing Him. The book of Hebrews describes such people as having a "fearful looking for of judgment and fiery indignation, which shall devour the adversaries" (Hebrews 10:27).

When I was a child, I frequently struggled with my grades in school. As such, I absolutely dreaded the days that report cards were sent home. Sometimes I would attempt to mitigate the inevitable punishment by feverishly doing chores like sweeping the garage or moving the lawn. In the end, however, these tasks did nothing to alleviate the inevitable wrath which was to come. It is a sad reality that we often approach God with the same mindset...We know that we have sinned, but we cling to the false hope that if we do enough good deeds, those works will hopefully make up for the evil things that we have done. In God's economy, however, this does not work. God is absolutely holy and must judge sin. Thankfully, He has already dealt with all of our sin through the death and resurrection of His Son, the Lord Jesus Christ who took the punishment and wrath for all the sins of all humanity upon Himself on the cross. We need only to receive that forgiveness by faith through a personal relationship with Him.

The fear of punishment brings condemnation which produces hopeless discouragement. Such discouragement only leads to apathy or rebellion, but a fear of God which is founded and grounded in love and awe will motivate us to trust Him. This paradox is seen throughout the Psalms, as exemplified in Psalm 40:3, which declares, "He put a new song in my mouth, a hymn of praise to our God. Many will see and fear and put their trust in the Lord." For those who are in a covenant relationship with God, it is not His desire that they cower with fear of His wrath. Hebrews 4:16 exhorts us, "Let us therefore come boldly unto the throne of grace, that we may obtain mercy, and find grace to help in time of need." Paradoxically, the New Testament still commands believers to have a fear of God. 1 Peter 2:17 contains four quick commands, including the command to "Fear God," but what does the fear of God look like to the believer?

In the original Hebrew text of the Old Testament, the root verb for fear is *yare*. Although the verb does often mean to tremble with fear, it also connotes other definitions, such as reverencing, honoring, and standing in awe of someone.[71] According to Lewis John Eron, Jewish writers have observed that in the Old Testament, the fear of God tends to be clustered with obedience to God, springing of a love for Him.[72] Ideally, we should fear God because we love Him and stand in awe of His magnificent power and glory. Eron goes on to observe that "God is deserving of humanity's respect because of God's great and magnificent deeds."[73] When we read of His marvelous works in the Word of God, we cannot help but respond in fearful amazement. When we witness the dramatic miracles of deliverance which He has brought about in our own personal lives, how much more shall we stand in awe of His wonder? The greatest awe-inspiring miracle of all is found in the way that He gloriously saved us from our former, destructive path of sin and death. The more we realize how utterly lost we were when we were separated from Him, the more we are compelled to fearfully worship Him for His glorious work of redemption and salvation.

The fear which we have toward God reveals the nature of our relationship with Him. Let us fear Him with a right heart, as His children who love Him, reverence Him, and stand in awe before His holiness for the great and mighty things which He has done—not only in the world, but in our personal journeys. What kind of fear do you have toward Him? Are you paralyzed with fear of His wrath, or do you stand in fearful amazement and wonder at His indescribable greatness? It is His longing desire that we step from the former fear in the kingdom of darkness into the latter fear which is found in the Kingdom of His Dear Son, the Lord Jesus Christ. *If you have not yet crossed the threshold into His loving presence, His free gift of grace and reconciliation is only a prayer away. Call upon Him today, and begin to experience the amazing fullness of His love and glory! He is eagerly waiting for you to respond to Him!*

PRAYER

Lord Jesus, I truly thank You for saving me through Your marvelous death and resurrection on my behalf. Please continue to reveal Your amazing love for me, so that I might not cower in fear of You, but that I might run to You. I stand in awe of Your glorious presence. I pray that You will continue to reveal Godly fear to me, and that Your Holy Spirit will help me to discern ungodly fear which is borne out of a spirit of condemnation.

I pray this in name of Jesus!

DECLARATION

I declare that I have a healthy, positive fear of God. I stand in awe and reverence of the glorious God and Creator of the universe, but I do not yield to an ungodly, condemning fear of punishment which would paralyze my relationship with Him. I declare that I am a child of God. I am His and He is mine. He will never leave me nor forsake me, and His love for me will never end. I come boldly to the Lord Jesus Christ in my times of need and I look for His wonder-working power to deliver me when I cry out to Him. I will declare His wonderful works to others so that all may fear and honor His holy name.

I declare this by faith in Jesus' name!

QUESTIONS

1. Do you have a healthy or an unhealthy fear of God? What does that fear look like?
2. What does your fear of God reveal about your relationship to the Father?
3. How has this devotional changed your understanding of the fear of God?

DAY 16

שִׂישׂ

siys

God Is Really, Really Excited Over Us!

> The Lord thy God in the midst of thee is mighty; he will save, he will rejoice over thee with joy; he will rest in his love, he will joy over thee with singing.
> – Zephaniah 3:17

Arguably, one of the most depressing Christmas carols ever written is "Oh Come, Oh Come, Emmanuel." Ironically, the stanzas were written to convey a sense of hope, but the message is somehow lost in translation. In spite of the exhortation to "Rejoice!" what was meant to be a song of joy instead comes across as a depressing funeral dirge. So it is with religious traditionalism which has created a false, twisted dichotomy between the restrained sense of joy which religion teaches us that God feels, and the human joy which we truly love to experience. While the secular meaning of joy involves exuberance and excitement, religious or spiritual joy has been reduced to little more than a sigh, a fake, condescending smile, and a religious folding of the hands. If we truly believe that we were created in the image of God, and indeed we were (Genesis 1:27), then how is it possible that our emotions have become so foreign to those of God, and His to ours?

Perhaps nowhere in the Bible is the overflowing, abundant nature of God's joy expressed more vividly than in Zephaniah 3:17. In its original context, this verse describes the excitement which the Lord will express in a future day when He will ultimately return and deliver His people Israel from all of her enemies. At the same time, it provides a glimpse of the immeasurable love of God which He feels toward His children who are in covenant relationship with Him.

How amazing is joy which overflows out of his abundant love toward us! When we look at ourselves through the prism of all of our faults, our shortcomings, our failures, and our weaknesses, we often have trouble believing that there is anything in us which is worthy of value—much less the love of God. To the contrary, this verse reveals how much God not only loves us in a generic or an obligatory sense (if these forms of love were even possible), but how much He is absolutely, completely, totally, crazily, madly, head-over-heels, insanely in love with each and every one of us—so much so that He cannot contain Himself each time He thinks of us!

If you have ever gone on a trip and tried to over-pack a suitcase with so many clothes that you had to put all your weight on it and maybe even jump on it to close it, you might begin to get a visual picture of the overflowing, exuberant, emotion which God feels toward us. This is the joy which Zephaniah attempts to convey within the bounds of one single verse. The Keil-Delitzsch Commentary observes, "The fullness [of the Lord's exuberance] is indicated in the heaping up of words for exulting and rejoicing."[74] The first Hebrew word encountered in this verse expresses that He will rejoice (or exult), translated from the Hebrew word *siys*.[75] The Strong's Concordance describes this word as being "bright" or "cheerful." Have you ever known a high-energy morning person who wakes up before everyone else and sings in the shower, to the annoyance of everyone else in the house? The Hebrew definition of *siys* likewise evokes images of such a bubbly person who is gushing over with happiness. It would be enough to end the sentence at this point, but the Hebrew goes on to say that the Lord will rejoice with "joy" (*simchah*).[76] This is the noun form of the verb *samach*, which means "to rejoice or be glad."[77] In a sense, this could also be rendered, "The Lord will rejoice over you with rejoicing," expressing a poetic form of emphatic redundancy.

As if the idea of rejoicing has not yet been exhausted, the text goes on to say that the Lord will "rejoice over you with singing." This time, the word for rejoicing is rooted in the Hebrew word *giyl*.[78] *Giyl* describes the outward expression of overflowing joy. Strong's

Concordance elaborates on the idea of spinning around. In modern Arabic there is a similar word which means "to go around or about" in excitement.[79] Several years ago, I received a check for five thousand dollars and was literally jumping and whooping for joy! I believe that the word *giyl* conveys the same idea of excitement which is impossible to contain! The verb *giyl* has also been translated as meaning "to cry shrilly"[80]. On one occasion while I was attending school in Tulsa, I had the privilege of attending an African wedding. What stood out to me the most about the wedding was that the entire ceremony was peppered with high-pitched cries of excitement from the women.

Zephaniah goes on to say that the Lord will rejoice with singing (King James Version, New International Version) or shouts of joy (New American Standard Bible). The Hebrew word does not easily translate to English; but the word used is *rinnah*, which means a "ringing cry."[81] The word is onomatopoetic, meaning it is a poetic word that is formed from a sound with which it is associated. When I was growing up, I spent a couple of summers up at my grandparents' home in northern Minnesota. The property was rather large and since my grandpa and I were usually working way out back in the woods, my grandma would ring an antique school bell which they used as a dinner bell. The word *rinnah* would be a good Hebrew word to describe the sound of the bell ringing. Metaphorically, "with a ringing cry" describes how the Lord will shout with glee over His beloved children. Taken altogether, Zephaniah 3:17 describes the totality of God's rejoicing over His people.

Nestled right in the middle is a line that is so contrary to the rest of the verse that it seems oddly out of place. When it is understood however, this adds an amazing dimension of God's loving passion toward us. Although the King James Version attempts to translate the expression to mean, "He will rest in His love," the root verb from which "rest" is translated is *charash*, which in this context is better interpreted to mean "to be silent or speechless."[82] This reveals God the Lover. When people fall in love, there are times when no words are necessary. The lovers love to draw close together and words become a noisome distraction. The same idea is being conveyed here. The Keil-Delitzsch Commentary describes it this way: "Silence in His love is an expression used to denote love deeply felt, which is absorbed in its object with thoughtfulness and admiration, and forms the correlate to rejoicing with exultation, *i.e.* to the loud demonstration of one's love."[83]

Do you feel unloved? Although you may often feel insignificant in the eyes of the world, you can be exuberantly enthralled in the knowledge that the God of the universe is truly in love with you! He does not merely tolerate you, nor does He simply love you in a wholesale, generic sense of the word; but He is absolutely consumed with a personal, burning passion for you! Bask in His love today!

PRAYER

Lord Jesus, I pray that You will reveal Your amazing love for me. I ask for this not merely on an cold, theological, intellectual level, but that I would understand in the depths of my heart the depth of the passion that You have for me. I pray that I will be so overwhelmed with the knowledge of Your love that it will overflow through me to everyone whom You have placed in my life. Let every thought that I think, every word that I speak, and everything that I do be ignited by Your passion.

I pray this in name of Jesus!

DECLARATION

I declare that I am a child of God. I am a child of the King. I am His and He is mine. He rejoices over me! He dances over me! He whoops and hollers over me; and He sings over me because He passionately loves me. I am so consumed with His infinite love that I, in turn, pour out His love to my friends, my family, my coworkers, and every person in my life.

I declare this by faith in Jesus' name!

Priceless Stones

QUESTIONS

1. In what ways has the devotional today increased your understanding of how much God really loves you?
2. Why do you think that there is a distorted difference between what we understand to be spiritual joy and human joy?
3. In what ways have we perhaps fallen short in effectively communicating the love of God to others, even when we were telling them about the gospel of Jesus Christ?

DAY 17

גבר

gabar

He Is the Mighty, Mighty God

Lift up your heads, O ye gates; and be ye lift up, ye
everlasting doors; and the King of glory shall come in.
Who is this King of glory? The Lord strong and mighty,
the Lord mighty in battle.
— Psalm 24:7-8

When I was a child, one of my favorite cartoon characters was Mighty Mouse. Although I will date myself here, I grew up on the Mighty Mouse of the 1950s and the 1960s, a superhero who was distinguished by his unusual fusion of crime-fighting ability and opera-singing talent. It seemed that no matter how urgent the crisis, Mighty Mouse was never in too much of a hurry to belt out an operetta as he was flying on the way to saving the world.

Sadly, pop culture has often usurped attributes which rightfully belong to God. One of those attributes is that of being "mighty," a description watered down by the proliferation of innumerable, imaginary superheroes which have been created over the years. By contrast, in the ancient Jewish culture, the mighty power of God evoked a sense of fear and awe and wonder at His glory and majesty. In Psalm 24:8, the Hebrew word used for mighty is *gibbor,* which is rooted in the verb *gabar,* which means, "to be strong, mighty;" or "to prevail (over)."[84] In the Hebrew text, there is a doubling of the consonants in the middle, which is used to convey an intensive form of the word; i.e., God is not just described as being mighty, which is awesome enough, but He is declared as **MIGHTY!**[85] If there is any room for doubt or confusion, the exact word is repeated in the same sentence for emphasis. The word *gibbor* is used extensively in the Old Testament and is associated with the following deeds and attributes of God:

- His righteousness and goodness.[86]
- His name (in rabbinical times, this word was used as a substitute for the proper name of God, as "The Name" is still used.) The name of the Lord was so holy that it was not to be uttered.[87]
- His actions in creation and in salvation toward His people.[88]
- His physical might, power, authority, and splendor.[89]
- His military accomplishments (also commonly used of men, as well), which is the most common use of the word.[90]

In biblical times, it was common among the pagan idolaters to participate in processions in which they would carry large statues of their gods into their temples. You have probably seen this in old period films about ancient Egypt or Rome. By surpassing contrast, Psalm 24:7-8 is communicating that the Lord is so overwhelmingly mighty and huge in stature that the top cornice over the doors or gates of the Temple would need to be removed in order for Him to enter.[91]

In general, many churches have a weak perception of the magnitude of the presence of God. While they may embrace the theology that God is everywhere, His presence is, in practice, confined to sanctuaries, shrines, tabernacles, or other physical locales. The reality is that God is indeed everywhere. Psalm 139:7-10 ponders His omnipresence: *"Whither shall I go from thy spirit? or whither shall I flee from thy presence? If I ascend up into heaven, thou art there: if I make my bed in hell, behold, thou art there. If I take the wings of the morning, and dwell in the uttermost parts of the sea; Even there shall thy hand lead me, and thy right hand shall hold me."* Moreover, Isaiah 40:12 paints a vivid picture of the scale of His might, declaring that it is the Lord *"Who hath measured the waters in the hollow of his hand, and meted out heaven with the span."*

In the New Testament, Matthew wrote the Gospel of Matthew for the purpose of explaining to His fellow Jewish countrymen that the Lord Jesus Christ was, and is, the promised Messiah who was foretold under the Old Covenant. Matthew does so by a variety of means—one of which is His documentation of the glorious miracles which Jesus did which could only be attributed to God Himself. Matthew refers specifically to the "mighty works" of Jesus more than any of the other gospel writers (see Matthew 11:20 21, 23; Matthew 13:54, 58; Matthew 14:2). When Matthew speaks of these mighty works, He does not simply use "mighty" as an exclamation, but He uses a word which His Jewish audience would have understood as describing what only God can do. Just as Jesus was in the business of healing, saving, and delivering His people, so He continues to do so today, because He is risen and He is the same yesterday, today, and forever (Hebrews 13:8).

The same Mighty God who created the heavens and the earth, and the same Mighty God who raised the Lord Jesus Christ from the dead stands ready to do mighty works on your behalf. Do you need healing? He is Mighty to heal. Do you need forgiveness? He is Mighty to cleanse. Do you need a financial miracle? He is Mighty to provide. Do you need salvation? He is Mighty to save. *Whatever you need today, He is more than enough...He is the great I AM, and He will be to you whatever you need Him to be. He loves you so much...call upon Him and watch Him demonstrate His amazing love and power in your life!*

PRAYER

Lord Jesus, I call upon You today. I thank You that absolutely nothing is impossible for You! There is nothing You cannot do! I bring my needs and desires to You today and put them in Your hands. I thank You that You continually show Yourself strong and mighty on my behalf.

I pray this in name of Jesus!

DECLARATION

I declare that I am a child of God. I am a child of the King and the Most High God! He is my Healer; He is my Provider; He is my Savior; He is my everything and my all in all. I confess that He not only hears my prayers, but that He moves mightily on my behalf. He makes the impossible possible. He is glorious and mighty to save. I choose, by an act of my will and by an act of my faith, to put my full trust in Him. He will do mighty works on my behalf, because He loves me.

I declare this by faith in Jesus' mighty name!

QUESTIONS

1. Having read this devotional, what new understanding do you have about the meaning of "mighty"?
2. What are the mighty works that God has done in your life?
3. What mighty works do you need from God today?

DAY 18

יֵשַׁע

yasha

He Miraculously Saves Us

He will fulfill the desire of them that fear him: he also
will hear their cry, and will save them.
— Psalm 145:19

When I was a child, our family used to go on a lot of camping trips. I remember one particular trip which we took to Florida when I was a teenager. I was swimming in the ocean and following my cousin as he was leading me further and further from the shore into waters which were well over my head. After a few moments, I lost track of where my cousin had gone and I suddenly found myself getting physically exhausted from fighting the large waves and the strong undertow. I then began to get frightened because I was not sure how much longer I could keep my head above water. Just in the nick of time, help arrived in the form of a friend who had been watching me from the beach. Having watched my struggling, he paddled out to me on a small, inflatable pool raft and brought me safely back to shore.

Many of us can recall at least one time when we were at wits' end and needed to be rescued. Even if we cannot think of a time when we were physically saved, those of us who have come to Christ have experienced a salvation no less dramatic—the saving of our very souls from eternal death. My ocean story is a powerful metaphor of how Satan gradually lures us away from God and abandons us to our own destruction at the very moment that we are overwhelmed by our sin. The enemy of our souls does not come to us with horns and a pitchfork as depicted in our culture, and he most certainly does not blatantly tell us to destroy our lives with drugs or alcohol or whatever our particular weakness may be. No, my friend! He gradually lures us, one baby step at a time, deeper and deeper into a life of bondage to sin. All the while he convinces us that we are still in control until we are suddenly overtaken and need to be rescued. Thankfully, the Lord is faithful and merciful. He does not reject us even after we have spurned Him for many years.

From Genesis to Revelation, the Bible is replete with testimonies to the saving power of God, who saves us on so many levels. In the Old Testament, the verb most commonly used, as in today's verse, is *yasha,* which is synonymous with rescuing, delivering, liberating, and of course, saving.[92] The Hebrew name of our Lord Jesus Christ is Y^{e}howshua (or "Joshua," the English form), which means, "The Lord has saved." So what are some ways that the Lord saves? The Bible provides many examples of His salvation, including the following: He delivers the poor man out of His troubles (Psalm 34:6); He liberates the slave (Psalm 107:12-13); and He frees the broken-hearted (Psalm 34:18). Most of all, He saves us from our sin (Ezekiel 36:29, Ezekiel 37:23; Isaiah 64:5-6; Jeremiah 4:14).[93]

Two thousand years ago, the Lord Jesus Christ paid the price to save us from our sin and from the curse of death. Through a personal relationship with Him, we have the marvelous privilege of being able to experience His salvation in our lives each and every day. Every time we call upon Him and give Him our troubles, our fears, our heartaches, and everything that bothers us and tries to rob us of our peace, He stands ever ready to deliver. I personally stepped into His wonderful saving grace in 1985, when I called upon the name of the Lord Jesus Christ in my own desperation and was freed from my bondage to a life of misery and rebellion.

In what ways have you experienced His saving power? If you cannot think of an answer to this question, perhaps you have not yet come to that point of surrender. If you have not, what is keeping you from crying out to Him for your deliverance? He ever waits to free us, to deliver us, to rescue us from our afflictions and to save us from our sin. *Call upon Him, and watch Him demonstrate His saving power in your life today!*

PRAYER

Lord Jesus, I come to You, completely helpless to save myself. I thank You for the salvation which You purchased with Your own precious blood. I thank You that, though the price of that salvation cost everything to You, You freely offer it to me as a gift. I come to You as a broken person and I thank You for forgiving me, healing me, delivering me, and making me whole.

I pray this in name of Jesus!

DECLARATION

I declare that I am a child of the Most High God. He hears my prayers, and He answers me when I call upon Him. He is my Savior; He is my Deliverer; He is my Liberator; He is my Healer. He faithfully rescues me from all my trouble and He causes me to triumph in Christ—not because of my own power and strength, but purely through His superior power and strength and because of His amazing mercy.

I declare this by faith in Jesus' name!

QUESTIONS

1. What is a testimony of the Lord's saving grace in your life?
2. What are some areas where you need His saving power?
3. What is keeping you from calling upon Him today?

DAY 19

שָׁלוֹם

shalom

He Is Our Abundant Peace

The Lord lift up His countenance upon thee,
and give thee peace.
– Numbers 6:26

Dr. Larry Hart, one of my beloved professors at Oral Roberts University, once joked, "School is like beating your head with a hammer: it feels so good when you stop!" We think of peace as being the absence of strife and war. It is well that we should, since this is one of the most commonly-used contexts in the Old Testament. The peace of God, however, is so much more all-encompassing than that!

The verse today is part of what is called the "Aaronic Blessing," found in Numbers 6:24-26. It is not merely a wishful prayer, but a prophetic declaration of blessing which the Lord gave to Moses during the wilderness wanderings. Moses was then to instruct the priests to speak this blessing over the Israelites, who were the Lord's chosen covenant people. Although this entire prayer is a rich declaration of blessing, we will focus on the promise of peace contained therein.

The word for peace, *shalom*, is one which is universally familiar to many, even to those having little or no knowledge of the Hebrew language. It is a common greeting in the Hebrew for "Hello!" and "Goodbye!"[94] In addition to the absence of strife or war, it also conveys the idea of completeness or wholeness, as well as harmony or fulfillment.[95] It is not merely a tentative peace in which one is fearfully waiting for the other shoe to drop at any moment, but an absolute sense of perfect, lasting security. Moreover, this peace is found not only in easy times, but is even available even in the midst of chaos. Psalm 29, which speaks of the awesome power of the voice of the Lord, describes one of the most vivid descriptions of terror found in the Bible, yet even in that psalm the writer concludes with the promise of *shalom* to those who love the Lord.

Shalom includes the promise of health, welfare, and prosperity.[96] When Joseph was reunited with his brothers, he inquired about the "welfare" of his father Jacob (Genesis 43:27).[97] The Hebrew word for welfare in this inquiry is the same word *shalom*. *Shalom* also speaks of enjoying perfect, unhindered relationships, both with God and with other people.[98] Several years ago, I attended a moving Messianic Jewish concert in which a former Palestinian-trained terrorist and an Israeli Jew embraced and blessed each other. This was a demonstration of the supernatural *shalom* which only God can give. Jesus said, "Peace I leave with you, my peace I give unto you: not as the world giveth, give I unto you" (John 14:27). He is foretold by the prophet Isaiah as the Prince of Peace (Isaiah 9:6), and indeed He is. Through the finished work of the Lord Jesus Christ, we who were once hostile enemies of God have been completely reconciled to Him (Colossians 2:21). There is no greater *shalom* than that!

Peace is a priceless gift which few people really encounter. Those whom we often look upon with envy because they seem to have all that the world has to offer are often disillusioned to find that the one thing that eludes them is peace. Peace cannot be purchased with money or gained by charm, but can only received by faith from God. Celebrities find themselves utterly dependent upon their physical appearance to satisfy their fickle fans and to maintain their fragile careers. Lottery winners are often bombarded by long-lost "relatives" hitting them up for money. On the other hand, the Bible promises, "The blessing of the Lord, it maketh rich, and he addeth no sorrow with it" (Proverbs 10:22). The Lord is good. He blesses us abundantly without the added sense of guilt that we are enjoying an abundance that others may not necessarily have. *Are you experiencing the peace of God in your life? If you are not, it is closer than you think! Call out to Him today, and freely receive the abundant shalom which He so* wants to give you! Do not keep it to yourself, but make it a lifestyle to bless your family members, friends, and every one you meet with His peace!

PRAYER

Lord Jesus, I thank You that You are the Prince of Peace. Fill my heart and my life today with Your peace alone that far surpasses all human comprehension. Let me experience every level of peace that only You have to offer. Let others see Your peace flowing like a mighty river through every area of my life, that You may be glorified and that people will be drawn to You because of Your overflowing, over-abounding goodness.

I pray this in name of Jesus!

DECLARATION

I declare that I walk day-by-day and moment-by-moment in the peace of God. It is not something that I work up by my own human effort; but rather, it is a fruit of the Holy Spirit who dwells in me. It is a gift from God. I choose to jealously guard my peace by clinging to the Lord Jesus Christ. He is my Rock; He is my Fortress; and He alone is my Shalom. I will not settle for any worldly counterfeits.

I declare this by faith in Jesus' name!

QUESTIONS

1. What is peace? What does it look like for your life?
2. Is anything robbing you of your peace today?
3. What are some biblical promises of peace which come to mind? Are you standing on those promises?

DAY 20

חָשַׁב

chashab

The Rope of Hope

For I know the thoughts that I think toward you, saith the Lord, thoughts of peace, and not of evil, to give you an expected end.
– Jeremiah 29:11

It is quite easy to believe that God has a plan for our lives when we feel that we have been good, but it is quite another matter to have this same confidence when we have been living in rebellion against Him. The scripture today is a glorious promise which was given to the nation of Israel at such a time. As we study this verse, we will experience a glimpse of His abounding, amazing grace which He lavishly pours out on our lives, even when we least deserve it.

The prophet Jeremiah was known as "the weeping prophet" because of the difficult message which he was called to deliver to the Israelites, recorded for all time in the book of Jeremiah, and its depressing sequel the book of Lamentations. Over the course of many generations, Israel had fallen from the former golden age of worship and blessing during the reigns of King David and his son Solomon, to being a divided kingdom whose heart had long since turned away from the Lord to the worship of pagan idols—even to the point of offering their children as sacrifices (Jeremiah 19:5) and worshipping bugs in the temple (Ezekiel 8:10). Prophet after prophet had been raised up by God to call the wayward nation to repentance, but with the exception of brief periods of revival, the hearts of the people had become set in stone in enmity against the very God who had once miraculously delivered them from slavery in Egypt and had brought them into the Promised Land.

In this setting, the message of Jeremiah was one of imminent, judgment upon the nation of Israel as well as the surrounding nations. Jeremiah's oracle was being undermined by those of competing false prophets who were promising that the Babylonian Empire, Israel's biggest threat, would quickly fall and that the Israelites would not be taken into captivity. In Jeremiah 29:10, the Lord told the Israelites that they would in fact be taken into captivity by the Babylonians, under whose yoke they would spend the next seventy years—an entire lifetime! Still, in the midst of all the impending doom and gloom, the Lord promised His people that His anger would not last forever. To the contrary, He still had a wonderful plan and a glorious purpose for them.

For I know the thoughts that I think toward you. The Hebrew word for "thought" is *machshaba*, from the root verb *chashab*, meaning "to think," but more precisely "to devise or to plan."[99] These are more than just passive thoughts—they are creative, devising thoughts of a specific future which the Lord is dreaming for His children. The same verb is used in Exodus 31:4 of the craftsman Bezaleel, who was gifted by God to artistically create beautiful items of gold, silver, and brass to be used in the service of the tabernacle.[100] When I young I remember how I used to toss and turn in bed all night, just thinking about future and what I wanted to do with my life. God is no less passionate about the plans that He has for us. He gets excited about how He wants to bless us—through our education, our future career(s), our mate, our children and even what he wants to do in *their* lives! Nothing is random to Him. He leaves nothing to chance. He has our whole life mapped out from cradle to grave and beyond—even millions of years into the future. As our heavenly Father, He has blessings which He wants to pour out on us which far exceed anything that we can dream on our own without Him. Not only does He have dreams for us, but He has all power to bring those dreams—even what seems impossible in our minds—to full fruition. We need only to trust Him and to give Him the reins and reign of our lives.

Jeremiah 29:11 concludes with the promise of an expected end. The King James Version is a weak translation and is better interpreted to mean "a future and a hope" as rendered in other versions. The last Hebrew word in the verse is *tiqvah,* which in its most basic form means "hope." Other nuances include "things hoped for," "outcome," or an "expected end."[101] Interestingly, the very same word is also translated to mean "cord."[102] The noun *tiqvah* is rooted in the verb *qavah*, "to wait for."[103] There are several Hebrew words for hope used in the Old Testament, of which this particular word is used less frequently. When it is used, it tends to be used in times of distress or affliction, when the petitioner is reminding himself of the hope of God's salvation (See also Psalm 71:5; Isaiah 40:31; Isaiah 51:5; Jeremiah 14:8; Jeremiah 17:13).[104] The idea is that, just as a rope is tightly twisted, taut, and tense, so was Israel to have the same posture in expectantly waiting upon the salvation of the Lord.[105]

When I was a child, I had a very brief tee ball career. I was usually stuck way out in left field, where my natural tendency was to allow the mind to daydream and wander; yet it was drilled into our little heads that we had to constantly be physically poised to run and catch the ball even when it was not coming in our direction. So ought we as believers to be of the same mind, expectantly waiting for the salvation of the Lord when we are passing through trials and tribulations and having our eyes and hearts fixed on heaven as we wait for the coming of the Lord Jesus Christ.

Every rope has an end. The rope may be so long that we may not be able to readily see it, but the end is there nonetheless. After all the suffering and affliction through which the Israelites were to pass, the end was not one of final destruction but one of hope and promise. Not only does hope pertain to an ethereal sense of bliss in a heavenly dimension, but Judah comments that this hope is one of material prosperity.[106]

While the original message of Jeremiah 29:11 was addressed to the wayward Israelites, it reveals the heart of God in such a way that it strikes a universal chord in every person. All of us pass through difficult times. Some of the most gut-wrenching circumstances are those that come about as a result of our own wrong-doing. It is in these times that we find it difficult, if not impossible, to forgive ourselves—let alone to believe that God could ever forgive us! The wonderful, biblical hope that we have is that God is merciful beyond our understanding. Regardless of what we have done, He never gives up on us. He never throws up His hands in despair and abandons us. In eternity past, He formulated a glorious plan for each of our lives which He never takes back. Although at the moment we may only be able to see the trees, God, from His heavenly perspective above, sees the entire forest.

At the cross, the Lord Jesus Christ paid the penalty for all the sins of every person who ever has walked, and ever will walk, the face of the earth. Sadly, when we have sinned, we have a tendency to run away from Him; but if we will turn to Him and cling to Him, regardless of what we have done and regardless of how long we have been doing it, He will not only freely forgive us, but He will bring about complete restoration in our lives. *Is your hope for a future fading, or has it perhaps been lost altogether? Give the Lord Jesus your worst past, and He will give you His best future!*

PRAYER

Lord Jesus, I thank You so very much for Your amazing grace, mercy and kindness. I am in awe of You that You love me so deeply that You have even laid out an amazing future of blessing for me that I cannot even begin to comprehend. I give You all of my sins and I thank You that every one of those sins—even the most awful, heinous, and unspeakable ones—have been completely washed away by Your precious blood that You freely poured out on the cross of Calvary in my place. I receive Your forgiveness and I look with eager anticipation to see what glorious plans that You are unfolding in my life. Take the reins of my heart and be Lord of my life.

I pray this in name of Jesus!

DECLARATION

I declare that the Lord Jesus Christ has a divine plan for my life. I have been cleansed of all sin and all unrighteousness through His blood that He shed for me. There is nothing that I can do that can thwart the purposes which God has ordained for me before the foundation of the world. Even when I have been in rebellion, God never gives up on me. That which He began in me, He will perform and complete it until the day of Jesus Christ.

I declare this by faith in Jesus' name!

QUESTIONS

1. What dreams has God placed in your heart?
2. Do you expectantly believe for those dreams to come to pass?
3. Who are some people in the Bible who saw the fulfillment of their dreams, long after they themselves might have given up on them?

DAY 21

חסד

cheçed

His Mercy Endures Forever

O Give thanks unto the Lord; for He is good:
for His mercy endureth forever.
– Psalm 136:1

In the United States, when we think of storks, we think of babies and pickles. In the Holy Land, however, the stork is renowned for two main attributes—its tenderness and its dependability. It is no coincidence that the Hebrew word for stork, *chaçiydah*,[107] is rooted in the same word as *cheçed*, meaning "mercy," "goodness," and "kindness."[108]

As with many other attributes of God, we have a limited understanding of His mercy. We tend to think of mercy only in terms of forgiveness of sins. While the mercy of God naturally includes His forgiveness, it goes far beyond that and encompasses all of His goodness which He lavishly pours out upon His creation—especially upon the people whom He has created in His image.

Psalm 136 is known in Judaism as "The Great Hallel." This psalm is a good place to meditate upon His goodness, mercy and kindness, because it reveals His care and faithfulness throughout the course of history. First, His goodness, mercy, and kindness are seen in His creation of the sun, the moon, and the stars (Psalm 136:4-9).[109] All of these things reflect His goodness, mercy, and kindness toward men because they affect life on earth. Think of how long we would be able to survive if the sun did not exist! The sun gives us light, warmth, and energy. Without the sun, all the plants would soon die, and all animal and human life would likewise perish. The moon and the stars give light at night, lest the world plunge into total darkness each night. Second, His goodness, mercy, and kindness are seen in His deliverance of Israel from slavery in Egypt, His care for them in the wilderness, and His bringing them into the Promised Land (Psalm 136:10-22).[110] Third, His goodness, mercy, and kindness are demonstrated by His works of redemption (Psalm 136:23-24).[111]

In its immediate context, the psalmist might have been specifically speaking of His redeeming Israel from her enemies; but because of what the Lord Jesus Christ has done for us, we have even more blessings for which we can be grateful. The Lord Jesus went to the cross in our place and took upon Himself the wrath of God for all the sins of all humanity. As a result, we no longer face an eternity of being separated from the Father, but we have been given the opportunity to live forever in His presence, cleansed of all sin and clothed in the righteousness of His dear Son. Fourth, His goodness, mercy, and kindness are shown in his care for His creation (Psalm 136:25).[112] One writer observed, "The entire world is the stage for the demonstration of Yahweh's kindness."[113]

The *Theological Dictionary of the Old Testament* highlights three characteristics of the c*heçed* of God: 1) it is active; 2) it is social; and 3) it is enduring.[114] By virtue of being "active," it goes beyond feelings and leads to action. Moreover, it intentionally pursues opportunities to bless others. One morning on the way to work, I stopped at a convenience store near the end of its shift change, when an employee was changing the trash bags on the gas pump islands. When the employee went inside, I grabbed the bags and took them to the dumpster. As silly as that sounds, God has called us to be a blessing wherever we go, so we can expect that He will ask us to do some strange things to demonstrate His love toward others. As we practice such acts of kindness, we can bring glory to Him through simple acts of service which anyone can do.

The social dimension of c*heçed* being social primarily involves direct acts of kindness toward people, which create or strengthen human relationships. It is directed more toward individuals than to cities, nations, or institutions. In the world system, there tends to be a focus on donating time, energy, or money to charitable organizations, which is a good thing; but the heart of God is to touch people on a personal level. God has the very hairs of our heads numbered. He knows the cries of our hearts, and some of the most powerful miracles He does are not so much via dramatic signs in the heavens, but by means of answers to secret prayers of which no one else is aware. The Lord Jesus Christ offered the ultimate act of sacrifice when He laid down His life on the cross for all humanity, but He did not stop there. He wants to be involved in our lives to love us and bless us on a deeply intimate level. While He mostly lavishes His love on us Himself, He also often chooses to express that love through other people.

In addition to being active and social, a third quality of God's *cheçed* is its ongoing nature. Many of us have seen the popular bumper sticker from several years back, suggesting that we "Practice random acts of kindness." While this may be a cheery message, it falls pathetically short of the mercy of God. It is God's very nature to love (1 John 4:8); God's goodness, grace, and kindness are not just infrequent acts which He occasionally bestows upon people when He happens to be in a good mood—these attributes are expressions of the very essence of who He is. God is good all the time, and He devotes every second of His time and every ounce of His energy to pouring out His blessing upon our lives—most often when we are unaware of what He is doing.

When I think about the goodness, mercy, and kindness which the Lord has shown toward me, I stand in awe at what an amazing, amazing God we serve. For the first twenty-one years of my life, I lived completely apart from God. Feeling all alone in the world, I was constantly depressed and tried to numb the pain of my miserable self esteem by a variety of means—whether it was drinking myself to drunkenness with my high school friends (what few I had) and later on with my Air Force friends, or whether it took the form of trying to prove my worth through awards which I earned during my brief military career. By the time I came to Christ, I had developed a foul mouth and a love of pornography; but God, who is rich in goodness, mercy, and kindness, never, ever stopped loving me despite the worm I had become. On November 2nd, 1985, He revealed Himself to me and instantly made me a brand new person—not just reformed, not just more disciplined, but thoroughly recreated from the inside out. He extends the same opportunity to every person who will simply call upon the name of the Lord Jesus Christ by faith (Romans 10:9-10, 13). *Have you personally experienced His goodness? If you have not, what is keeping you from embracing His love today? Open up your heart to Him, and let Him flood you with His amazing grace!*

PRAYER

Lord Jesus, I thank You from the bottom of my heart for Your ongoing goodness, grace and kindness. I am Your child, made in Your image. Please help me everyday to pour out Your goodness to those around me. Open my eyes continually to opportunities to brighten the lives of other people and to lighten their burdens. Let Your love flow through me like a river, not only in my thoughts and attitudes, but in my words and actions.

I pray this in name of Jesus!

DECLARATION

I declare that God is a good God. He is not against me—He loves me deeply and He is for me! I choose to thank Him and praise Him for His goodness. I choose not to dwell on what I do not have, but upon what He has given to Me. His goodness, His grace, His love, His mercy, and His kindness so flood my being, that I cannot help but give these things away to others- even to those who do not show these things in return. I am a child of God, so I reflect His glory everywhere I go, toward every person whom I encounter.

I declare this by faith in Jesus' name!

QUESTIONS

1. What are some examples of God's goodness which you have seen in your own life?
2. How has the devotional today expanded your awareness or understanding of the mercy of God?
3. What are some specific ways that you can demonstrate the goodness, mercy, and kindness of God to others?

DAY 22

היה

hayah

He Is the Amazing I AM

> And Moses said unto God, Behold, when I come unto the children of Israel, and shall say unto them, The God of your fathers hath sent me unto you; and they shall say to me, What is his name? What shall I say unto them? And God said unto Moses, I AM THAT I AM: and he said, Thus shalt thou say unto the children of Israel, I AM hath sent me unto you.
> – Exodus 3:13-14

All of us have some form of identity in this world. When we first meet someone, we may describe ourselves by saying, "I am…" and fill in the blank. Only the Lord God, however, can say of Himself, "I AM," and leave it at that. When we come to an understanding of the impact of this statement, it will send shivers down our spine. Demons tremble in the presence of God (James 2:19); prophets fall on their face when they see the glory of God (Ezekiel 1:28; Revelation 1:17); and there is coming a day when every knee shall bow and every tongue shall confess that Jesus Christ is Lord to the glory of God the Father (Philippians 2:10-11).

The verse today refers to Moses' life-changing encounter with the Lord at the burning bush. During this encounter, the Lord declares that He is about to lead the children of Israel out of slavery in Egypt through mighty signs and wonders. When Moses asks whom he shall say has sent Him, the Lord simply responds the he is to tell the Israelites that "I AM that I AM" has sent him.

Throughout the Old Testament, the unutterable name of the Lord, *Y^{e}hovah,* is derived from the Hebrew verb *hayah* which simply means "to be" or "to become."[115] In 1520, the name *Y^{e}hovah* was transliterated into Jehovah in the English language by the Christian scholar Petrus Galatinus.[116] Dr. William McDonald, Professor of Old Testament at Oral Roberts University said it best when he defined it to mean, "I will be whoever you need me to be!"[117]

The name of the Lord was considered so holy that its very utterance was forbidden, and continues to be to this day in Orthodox Judaism. As a result of its forbidden utterance, the original pronunciation was lost over the centuries and still remains unknown.[118] To this day, out of awesome reverence for this name, *Y^{e}hovah* is neither pronounced nor fully written in orthodox Jewish culture, but is customarily replaced by other titles which are understood to refer to the Lord, such as *Adonai* or *Hashem,* meaning, "The Name." As the Lord progressively reveals Himself in the Old Testament, the Scripture often couples *Y^{e}hovah* (He is or He shall be) with specific attributes to reveal His nature. For example, *Jehovah-Shalom* (*Y^{e}hovah-Shalowm*) means, "The Lord is peace;"[119] or more literally, "He is/He shall be Peace" (Judges 6:24).

In revealing Himself as "I AM," the Lord highlights His ongoing presence.[120] To say "I was" or "I shall be" might have left Moses or the reader to wonder how the Lord could be near if He only called to remembrance His faithfulness in the past or made a promise to assist in the future. "I AM" always refers to the present moment. The psalmist sang, "God is our refuge and strength, a very present help in trouble" (Psalm 46:1). What a wonderful comfort to know that He is always near when we call upon Him!

The glorious, mighty power of His name cannot be overstated. I could not possibly express it better than one commentator who wrote the following description:

> There is no doubt that the name, whatever its original meaning and use may have been, came to designate for Moses and for Israel the

living, self-existent God, the One who is and will be, and who has within himself the exhaustless resources of being. He is not define by one event, or by one circumstance, or by the experience of one age or nation, but is ceaselessly renewing the revelation of himself in the world of nature and in human history. His being is expressed in action. He will be with his people, guide, counselor, warrior, lawgiver, and mighty deliverer.[121]

While on the surface it seems as if the Lord is cryptically speaking to Moses in circles, "I AM that I AM" is written in a Hebrew grammatical construction called *idem per idem*. In this construction, a phrase is stated in a sentence as an independent clause and then repeated as a dependent clause in the same sentence for the sake of emphasis. This emphatic repetition expresses totality or intensity.[122] This type of expression is found in several places in the Old Testament—most notably, Exodus 33:19, where the Lord declares, "I will show compassion on whom I will show compassion."[123] In the spirit of this construction, Walter Kaiser translates this expression to mean, "I am truly he who exists and who will be dynamically present then and there in the situation to which I am sending you."[124]

Whether in first-person or third-person, the Scripture continues to declare the name of the Lord in this way on several more occasions in the Old Testament (See Deuteronomy 32:39; Isaiah 43:10, 13; Isaiah 44:5-6; Isaiah 48:12). Today there are many unbelieving scoffers who say that the Lord Jesus Christ never claimed to be God; but in the New Testament, specifically the Gospel of John, Jesus clearly declares Himself to be the same "I AM" (See John 8:24, 28, John 8:58; John 13:19; John 18:5-8). For this very reason, the Jewish leaders of Jesus' day attempted to stone Him (John 8:59). The Bible testifies that, on the night of Jesus' arrest, the people drew back and fell to the ground when He declared, "I AM" (John 18:6). Many of the verses in John do say, "I am *he*," but do not be confused! In several versions of the Bible, most notably the King James Version, the word "*he*" is in italics. This means that the italicized word was not in the original text, but was added by the translators for what they thought was needed clarification. For further testimony of the divinity of the Lord Jesus

Christ, the Book of Revelation refers to Him in the same manner (Revelation 1:4, 8; Revelation 4:8; Revelation 16:5).

When we think of the Lord as the "I AM," we sometimes tend to think of Him as being a distant God who created the universe but is now enthroned in heaven far away from our day-to-day reality. We read of the miracles that He did in the Bible, but we do not always believe that He truly wants to show His power in a very intimate way in each and every one of our daily lives, but He truly does! Shortly after I became a Christian, I was driving some friends up into the mountains on a Christmas night, for what was supposed to be a short drive from Colorado Springs to a nearby town. Somehow I missed a turn and we ended up getting hopelessly lost. We did not have much gas to begin with, and what few gas stations we did pass were all closed because of the holiday. It was late at night, the mountain roads were very dark, and the towns we encountered were few and far between. We were really getting scared that we were going to run out of gas in the middle of nowhere. When the tank got down to vapors, all of us in the car prayed in agreement for the Lord's help. Immediately as we were praying, the gas gauge rose before our very eyes to about one-fourth of a tank, which was enough to finally get us to a gas station that was open.

What desperate need do you have in your life today? You may have been diagnosed with AIDS or cancer or some other terminal disease...He is the "I AM" who can heal you! You may be on the verge of bankruptcy or foreclosure...He is the "I AM" who can provide for you! You may be going through an ugly divorce or a broken relationship...He is the "I AM" who can bring reconciliation! There is no miracle too big or too small for Him to demonstrate His power and the amazing, infinite love that He has for you! Oral Roberts always used to say, "Expect a miracle!" *Do you need to experience His glorious, miraculous, wonder-working, power today? Call out to Him today, and watch Him do amazing things in your life!*

PRAYER

Lord Jesus, I thank You that You are my God; You are the great I AM, and there is nothing You cannot do…Nothing is impossible for You. I am calling out to You today to move mightily in my desperate need. I thank You that You will take my turmoil and turn it into a testimony so that others will see Your goodness.

I pray this in name of Jesus!

DECLARATION

I declare that the God whom I love is the great I AM. He created the heavens and the earth and everything that is in them. He deeply loves me and He longs to show His love through mighty signs and wonders that He desires to do in my life. Nothing is impossible for Him; He can do all things. He did awesome miracles in biblical times, and He will do the same in my own life today.

I declare this by faith in Jesus' name!

QUESTIONS

1. What does the name "I AM" mean to you?
2. What are some miracles that you need in your life that only the "I AM" can do?
3. In what ways has your faith been increased today?

DAY 23

ראה

ra'ah

He Is Our Provider

> And Abraham called the name of that place Jehovah-Jireh: as it is said to this day, In the mount of the Lord it shall be seen.
> – Genesis 22:14

In yesterday's devotional, we saw how God is the great "I AM." In Him is everything that we will ever need, both in this present life and in the age to come. Given that reality, I think that it would be a tremendous encouragement to look at some of the specific biblical revelations of His name which highlight who He is and who He wants to be in our lives. We begin today with the revelation of *Adonai-Yireh*, whom we know as *Jehovah-Jireh* in our English vernacular.

This revelation of the Lord's name comes about in the Book of Genesis after Abraham offers his son Isaac on the altar. After the Angel of the Lord intervenes and stops Abraham from plunging the knife into Isaac, Abraham looks around and sees a ram caught in a nearby thicket which he then sacrifices to the Lord in place of his son. In honor of the Lord's miraculous provision of the ram, Abraham calls the place "*Jehovah-Jireh*," which roughly translates, "The Lord will provide." It was this very same mountain, Mount Moriah, that the Lord would chose to have the Temple built in the midst of what would later become the city of Jerusalem (See Genesis 22:2; 2 Chronicles 3:1).

In Christian circles, we have sung for years about *Jehovah-Jireh* being our Provider. He faithfully provides for our needs according to his riches in glory by Christ Jesus, as the Scripture promises

(Philippians 4:19). Whenever I am in an airplane looking down over the earth, I am reminded of how the Lord sees our lives from His heavenly perspective. Although the drivers in the cars below can only see that which is immediately in front of them, I, from my vantage point in the sky, can see miles ahead of them. So is it with the Lord. Because of His infinite foreknowledge, He knows the whole span of our lives from cradle to grave and beyond. Not only does He anticipate our future needs, but He is the One who sees ahead and makes provision for those needs, even when we are unaware that He is working on our behalf for our greatest good.

While I was a student at Oral Roberts University, I came to a point of desperation when I had completely run out of food in my apartment and had no money to buy groceries. Being a very private individual, I said nothing to anyone but prayed and believed God that He would supernaturally provide for me. On that very same day, a fellow student called and told me to come immediately to her home. When I arrived, she had bags and bags of groceries waiting for me! She had just gone grocery shopping that day for her family when the Lord told her to bless me with half of what she had purchased. I was overwhelmed to tears by her amazing generosity, and even more so that the very God of the universe would be so intimately aware of and concerned about my situation.

In the context of Genesis 22:14, the revelation of the name of *Adonai-Yireh* cuts to the very core of the deepest need that we will ever have—the essential need for forgiveness and redemption. *Jireh* is an English transliteration of the Hebrew word *yireh*, which is the future form of the verb *ra'ah*, meaning "to see."[125] In this sense, "to see" means "to provide for." In the English language, the expression "to see to something" used to be a way of expressing the idea, "to provide for a need."[126]

In the same way that the Lord provided the ram needed for a sacrifice for Abraham, so has the Lord provided through His Son, the Lord Jesus Christ, the final sacrifice for sin that we need in order to be forgiven of all of our sins and to be reconciled to Him. Colossians 1:21-22 tells us, "And you, who once were alienated and enemies in your mind by wicked works, yet now He has reconciled in the body of

His flesh through death, to present you holy, and blameless, and above reproach in His sight" (NKJV).[127] At one time we were lost in sin, without any hope of ever being able to earn the forgiveness of God. We were absolutely, utterly, completely, hopelessly, helpless to save ourselves. Nevertheless, the Lord Jesus Christ came and took upon Himself in His own body the wrath and punishment for the sins of every person who has ever lived, and who will ever be born. In the same way that the Lord miraculously provided the ram for Abraham, so has He miraculously provided the Lamb on our behalf.

It is one thing to have a mental construct of what the Lord Jesus Christ accomplished for us on the cross, but it is so much greater to *personally* experience His cleansing forgiveness! This alone is the faith that truly saves and transforms us. As the born-again children of God, we have the opportunity to experience this cleansing every single day if we will simply come worshipfully into His presence. The writer of the Book of Hebrews exhorts us, "Let us therefore come boldly unto the throne of grace, that we may obtain mercy, and find grace to help in time of need" (Hebrews 4:16).

The greatest turning point in my life occurred on November 2nd, 1985, the night that I gave my heart fully to Jesus Christ and made Him the Lord of my life. I had recently begun attending a church in Colorado Springs and was attending a weekend retreat in the Sangre de Cristo (which in Spanish means "Blood of Jesus") Mountains of Colorado with some new friends whom I had just met. On the first night of the retreat, an evangelist proclaimed the gospel message and invited those to who did not know Christ to come to the altar. Now I had thought I was a good person and that everything was fine between God and me; but as the moments wore on I felt the increasing conviction of the Holy Spirit tugging on my heart, revealing to me that all was *not* well between us. The speaker gave three successive calls, and by the supernatural word of knowledge declared with increasing intensity that there were people in the room who needed to get right with God. Although out of pride I initially resisted the Holy Spirit, I had such an overwhelming sense that I was one of those people that I finally *ran* to the front of the room! Although at that point no one explained the gospel to me nor led me through a sinner's prayer, it was nonetheless a point of surrender that forever changed my life and my eternal destiny. I have never gone back to being the same person that I was before that point in time.

Jeremiah 17:5-7 contrasts the cursedness of trusting in man and the contrasting blessedness of trusting in the Lord. *Who are you trusting today? Call upon the Lord today! He stands ready to meet your needs and to show Himself strong, mighty, and abundant on your behalf!*

PRAYER

Lord Jesus, I lift up the needs that I have before You this day. I thank You that You are all-knowing and all-powerful and You have already looked ahead and abundantly provided for those needs. I choose this day to trust wholeheartedly in You, and I thank You for Your supernatural provision. I thank You in advance for the amazing testimony that I continually have of Your faithfulness and loving-kindness.

I pray this in name of Jesus!

DECLARATION

I declare that God is able to make all grace abound toward me. I declare that I, always having all sufficiency in all things, may abound to every good work (2 Corinthians 9:8). I confess that He is able to do exceedingly, abundantly, above all that I could ask or think, according to His power that works within me (Ephesians 3:20). He is a good God, He is the mighty God, and He continually provides for every need that I will ever have- whether it be physical, financial, emotional, spiritual, or whatever the need may be. He is able!

I declare this by faith in Jesus' name!

QUESTIONS

1. What needs do you have in your life today?
2. Recall a specific time that the Lord supernaturally provided for you.
3. What are some other scriptures that come to mind which promise of the Lord's provision for you?

DAY 24

רפא

raphah

He Is Our Healer

> And said, If thou wilt diligently hearken to the voice of the Lord thy God, and wilt do that which is right in his sight, and wilt give ear to his commandments, and keep all his statutes, I will put none of these diseases upon thee, which have brought upon the Egyptians: for I am the Lord that healeth thee.
> – Exodus 15:26

One of the truths about the Lord that so often seems to bring offense is not that He is holy and righteous, but that He the God who heals. Those who are most hostile to this reality are not so much the unbelievers in the world system, but rather, church-going people who profess to know God. For centuries, many rationalistic, religious theologians have dedicated their professions to attempting to disprove this simple, life-giving reality.

We are currently focusing on the revealed names of God, and today we are beholding the name of *Adonai-Raphah* (*Yahveh-Raphah*, or *Jehovah-Raphah*). This revelation takes place in the wake of the Israelites' exodus from the land of Egypt. Having just crossed the Red Sea where they had witnessed the miraculous destruction of the pursuing Egyptian army, the Israelites encountered a test in which they had travelled three days through a desolate, desert wilderness without any water. Imagine their crushing disappointment when all the water before them ended up being foul! It was then that Moses cried unto the Lord and the Lord in response directed Moses to throw a tree into the water, which made it turn sweet. This miraculous healing of the water was turned into a sign of the Lord's healing power. In the same way that the Lord healed the foul water, He declared not only a promise, but a decree that He would not bring upon the Israelites the diseases which He had brought upon the Egyptians, for He is the God who heals.

The Hebrew verb used in this verse is *raphah*, which simply means "to heal."[128] A modern descendent Arabic word means "to mend" or "to repair," and likewise a modern Ethiopian word means "to stitch together"[129] To further reinforce the idea that this word specifically refers to physically healing, the *Theological Dictionary of the Old Testament* succinctly concurs with the conclusion of A. B. Erlich that, "Careful analysis of the OT materials shows, however, that *rp'* is used in every instance with reference to restoring a wrong, sick, broken, or deficient condition to its original and proper state."[130] It is the very same word used in Psalm 103:3, which explicitly declares without any ambiguity, "Who forgiveth all thine iniquities; who healeth all thy diseases." Moreover, the same verb is also used in Isaiah 53:5, which promises, "And with his stripes we are healed."

Some have attempted to neuter the Isaiah 53 passage to remove all references to physical healing, but even the Holy Spirit interprets this chapter to specifically apply to the healing of sickness and disease. Matthew, under the inspiration of the Holy Spirit, testifies in Matthew 8:16, "When the even was come, they brought unto him many that were possessed with devils, and he cast out the spirits with his word, and healed all that were sick." Immediately following in Matthew 8:17, Matthew points out that this was a fulfillment of what the prophet Isaiah had foretold in Isaiah 53:4, as he reminds the reader, "That is might be fulfilled which was spoken by Esaias the prophet, saying, Himself took our infirmities, and bare our sicknesses."

In John 14:9, The Lord Jesus Christ said to Philip, "He that hath seen me hath seen the Father." What do we see Jesus doing throughout the gospels? He is healing, healing, healing! Therefore, we know, based on the words of Jesus that it is the heart of the Father to heal us! When we come into a relationship with the Father through His Son, the Lord Jesus Christ, we enter into a covenant of health, healing and wholeness. Not only do we receive healing in our own bodies, but the

Holy Spirit comes and lives within us and His healing power flows through us to bring healing to others. Jesus promised of those who belong to Him, "They shall lay hands on the sick, and they shall recover" (Mark 16:18). This reality has been proved to be true more times than I can possibly count over the course of living in relationship with Christ for many, many years.

Many years ago when I was in the Air Force, I worked the graveyard shift for about two and a half years. One night, one of the government contractors came hobbling in on crutches and was obviously in a lot of pain. When I asked her what had happened, she told me that she had fallen off her horse in such a way that she had twisted both of her ankles and that she would be on crutches for about six weeks. I felt like the Holy Spirit was impressing upon my heart to pray for her, so during my lunch break she let me lay hands on her ankles. Within three days, she was completely healed and walking normally without any crutches!

In the fourth chapter of the Gospel of Luke, the Lord Jesus Christ proclaimed of Himself, "The Spirit of the Lord is upon me, because he hath anointed me to preach the gospel to the poor; he hath sent me to heal the brokenhearted, to preach deliverance to the captives, and recovering of sight to the blind, to set at liberty them that are bruised, to preach the acceptable year of the Lord" (Luke 4:18-19). *Where do you need healing? In your body? In your mind? In your emotions? In your relationships? He heals on so many levels. Call upon Him today, and let His healing power flow mightily and gloriously into your life!*

PRAYER

Lord Jesus, I thank You that Your Word promises that by Your stripes I have been healed. I receive Your power in my body, wherever I need it today. I thank You for the awesome testimonies of Your healing virtue which You are continually bringing about as I call upon Your name and trust in You as my Healer and Physician.

I pray this in name of Jesus!

DECLARATION

I declare that by Jesus' stripes I have been healed. The Lord Jesus Christ took every sickness, illness, disease, and infirmity upon Himself on the cross, so I do not have to tolerate sickness, pain or infirmity in my life. I therefore walk in divine health, healing, wholeness and restoration. Not only do I walk in divine health, but I carry the healing power of God to others, because the Holy Spirit dwells in me. I lay hands on the sick and they recover because the healing virtue of the Lord Jesus Christ flows through me like a mighty river.

I declare this by faith in Jesus' name!

QUESTIONS

1. What healing do you or your loved ones need today?
2. Recall a time that you witnessed a miraculous healing from the Lord.
3. What other scriptures can you think of that bear witness to the healing power of God?

DAY 25

שָׁם

sham

Wherever You Are, He Is There

It was round about eighteen thousand measures: and the name
of the city from that day shall be, "The LORD is there."
– Ezekiel 48:35

Several years ago, I was driving home to Colorado on a Christmas Eve night from a trip to Mexico. I had just passed through San Antonio when my car broke down near a town called Comfort, Texas. Being a holiday evening, this mechanical breakdown had all the elements of a perfect storm of aloneness. I could not reach anyone on the phone, I had very little money, I could not find an available mechanic, and I was supposed to be back at work in Colorado the day after Christmas.

After making my rounds to about four nearby convenience stores, I came to one final store where the clerk happened to know of an elderly gentleman who operated a small repair shop out of his garage. The next morning I was able to reach the gentleman but his truck did not have enough power to tow me to his garage, so I would need to drive under my vehicle's own power to his home. Although my engine had long since quit hours before, I prayed a quick prayer, turned the key, and the engine roared to life.

When I reached the elderly man's home, I felt like I had entered into a different dimension of time in an old black and white episode of "The Twilight Zone." The mechanic, who was probably about eighty years old, was scolding his grandson because the fire had gone out in the old wood stove in the garage. Despite the rustic conditions, he had my car repaired within thirty minutes...The problem? I had had some work done on the carburetor prior to the trip, but the previous mechanic had put in a new bolt that was too short. The elderly mechanic did not even want to charge me for the repair, but I ended up giving him thirty dollars—as much as I could afford at the time—because I felt I should give him something! After driving all day and all night, I made it to work on time as scheduled the day after Christmas.

I cannot think of a better real-life parable of the faithful presence of God than the testimony which was borne out of my trial in Comfort, Texas. When we have nowhere else to turn, what a comfort to know that the Lord is there and ready to rescue us from our distress! Although the revealed name of the Lord, *Adonai-Shammah*, in its original biblical context refers to the city of Jerusalem, it nonetheless reminds us that wherever we are, we are never outside the bounds of His presence. The psalmist David wrote, "Whither shall I go from thy spirit? Or whither shall I flee from thy presence? If I ascend up into heaven, thou are there: if I make my bed in hell, behold, thou are there" (Psalm 139:7-8).

Shammah is rooted in the common Hebrew adverb *sham*, which simply means "there."[131] As encouraging as this may be, it still falls short of the promise that the Lord is not only present, but that He is always with us. In Isaiah 7:14 and Isaiah 8:8, the prophet Isaiah reveals to us the name *Immanuel*, of which we sing during the Christmas season. *Immanuel* is a Hebrew compound word made up of three root words: *Im*, meaning "with"; *anu*, meaning "us";[132] and *El*, meaning "God."[133] The name, therefore, is best translated, "With us is God!"[134] To the Israelites, this was more than a simple intellectual understanding of the presence of God; it was a declaration of absolute trust and confidence in the God who is with us! It was a triumphant declaration that God is with us![135] King David boldly declares, "The Lord is on my side: I will not fear: what can man do unto me?" (Psalm 118:6) We, too, as believers in the Lord Jesus Christ, can go into any situation with the same boldness and confidence, trusting God that He is always with us, and that He is always there to defend us and take care of us. *What are you facing today? Remember that you are not alone. Trust in the Lord and take Comfort in knowing that He is truly with you!*

PRAYER

Lord Jesus, I thank You that You are the Almighty God. I thank You that You cause me to triumph in all things. I give You my cares and my worries, and I thank You in advance for the victory that You will give to me, and that that victory will bring praise and glory to Your name.

I pray this in name of Jesus!

DECLARATION

I declare that God is continually with me wherever I go. I cannot possibly escape from His presence. He is always ready and eager to save me every time I call upon His name. If God is for me (and He is!) who can be against me? (Romans 8:31) The Word of God promises that the Lord will never, ever leave me nor forsake me (Hebrews 13:5). I choose to walk in the reality that He goes before me, and that He watches over every detail and every need in my life.

I declare this by faith in Jesus' name!

QUESTIONS

1. Can you recall a time that you ever felt all alone? Ask the Lord to show you His presence when you were in that situation.
2. What are you facing today?
3. Do you truly believe that the Lord is present in your life today and that He is in complete control?

DAY 26

נֵס

nes

He Is Our Victorious Banner

And Moses built an altar, and called the name
of it Jehovah-Nissi.
– Exodus 17:15

When I was in Air Force basic training many years ago, I remember that the most coveted duty was that of being the flag bearer in the drill formations. There are few inanimate objects that can stir the soul and rally people together like a flag. Think of images like Iwo Jima and the iconic 9/11 photograph of the American flag being hoisted over the rubble of the World Trade Center.

The devotional today is based on the biblical account of the Israelites' first battle in the wilderness after the Egyptian army was drowned in the Red Sea. Exodus 17 describes how the Amalekites, a tribe of nomadic pillagers, attacked the Israelites in the wake of their freedom from slavery. Being yet unarmed and untrained for battle, the Israelites were quite defenseless and particularly vulnerable to attack from their more experienced, battle-hardened neighbors. The gold and silver which the Israelites had "borrowed" from the Egyptians during their exodus made them a very attractive target to their enemies.

Exodus 17:10-13 narrates how, when Moses lifted his hands, the Israelites prevailed; but when his hands grew tired and fell, the Amalekites prevailed. Aaron and Hur therefore set him down on a rock and held up his hands, and under the leadership of the up and coming Joshua, the Israelites won the battle. After the Lord told Moses to record the event in remembrance of His faithfulness, Moses built an altar and called it *Jehovah-Nissi (Y^{e}hovah-Nicciy)*, meaning, "The Lord is my banner or standard."[136] The Hebrew root noun of *nissi* is *nes*, meaning standard, ensign, signal, or sign.[137] It is derived from the verb *naças*, which means "to be high or conspicuous."[138] While the word *nes* has different functions throughout the Old Testament, in this context Moses builds an altar and names it *Jehovah-Nissi* for two purposes: 1) as a conspicuous declaration of ongoing war against the marauding Amalekites; and at the same time, 2) as a commemoration of victory.[139]

Communication has always been vitally important to the success of any military campaign. Long before the days of radio, telephone, and satellites, the primary means of battlefield communication was visual, through the means of large banners or standards. Amidst the chaos of smoke and advancing troops, banners were used in ancient times to mark places of assembly or to point in the direction of attack.[140] Moreover, a standard was planted as a claim of possession over a conquered or soon-to-be conquered city or territory.[141] Such banners often depicted pictures of the nations' god(s).[142] As such, the banner was a symbolic advancement of the god(s) into battle.[143]

Although the use of the banner or standard is never mentioned in connection with any of the Old Testament battle narratives, it is frequently used metaphorically to describe the mighty, triumphant God who gives victory to His people.[144] The prophet Isaiah describes the Lord Jesus Christ as our banner. Isaiah 11:10 promises, "And in that day there shall be a root of Jesse, which shall stand for an ensign of the people; to it shall the Gentiles seek: and his rest shall be glorious."[145] Like so many other promises, the Lord Jesus Christ does not only *give* us victory, He *is* our victory! That victory is the very essence of who He is!

We need not wait until the coming Messianic Age to experience that victory! The Lord Jesus Christ triumphed over all the powers of darkness when He rose from the dead, having paid the penalty in full for our sins when He died on the cross. The Apostle Paul proclaims, "And having spoiled principalities and powers, he made a shew of them openly, triumphing over them in it" (Colossians 2:15). We as born-again believers walk in that victory, not by the strength of our intellect or our natural abilities but purely by faith in Him. The Apostle John declares, "For whatsoever is born of God overcometh the world, and this is the victory that overcometh the world, even our faith. Who is he that overcometh the world, but he that believeth that Jesus is the Son of God?" (1 John 5:4-5).

You might ask, "Over what does He give us victory?" The answer is quite simple—everything that this world and the enemy possibly can throw at us! Galatians 3:13 heralds, "Christ hath redeemed us from the curse of the law, being made a curse for us." Everything that sin brought into the world—sickness, poverty, destitution, demonic attack and oppression and of course sin itself—was defeated at the cross. Granted, we still see and live in the midst of these things but the Lord Jesus has nonetheless given us all power and authority to overcome these things as His sons and daughters by faith in Him.

President Franklin Delano Roosevelt declared in his most famous speech, "We have nothing to fear but fear itself." I submit that I would take that further and boldly proclaim, "We have nothing to fear. Period." Philippians 2:9-10 tells us, "Wherefore God also hath highly exalted him, and given him a name which is above every name: that at the name of Jesus every knee should bow, of things in heaven, and things in earth, and things under the earth." *What battles are you facing today? I encourage you today to plant the banner of faith in that situation, and to expect the victorious power of Almighty God to triumph, no matter how overwhelming the trial may be. He is Jehovah-Nissi–the Lord our Victory! Stand and believe on Him that He will do great and mighty things!*

PRAYER

Lord Jesus, I think You that You are Jehovah-Nissi. You truly are my victory. I trust in You today and I thank You that You cause me to triumph in all things. I will boldy declare Your victory in whatever I am facing this week—in my job, in my finances, in my relationships, or wherever the trial may be. Thank you for the all-encompassing victory that You purchased through Your death and resurrection at Calvary.

I pray this in name of Jesus!

DECLARATION

I declare that I can do all things through Christ who strengthens me. Christ is my Lord. Christ is my King. He the Almighty God. I belong to Him and I will lay hold of His victorious power in every area of my life. I will not succumb to despair and discouragement because I belong to the Lord Jesus Christ, who is Jehovah-Nissi, the Lord my Victory.

I declare this by faith in Jesus' name!

QUESTIONS

1. What trials are you facing in your life today?
2. Recall a time when the Lord gave you a major victory.
3. What other promises of victory can you recall from Scripture? How are you steadfastly standing on those promises?

DAY 27

צבא

tsabah

He Is the Mighty Lord of Hosts

> Then said David to the Philistine, Thou comest to me with a sword, and with a spear, and with a shield: but I come to thee in the name of the Lord of hosts, the God of the armies of Israel, whom thou hast defied.
> – 1 Samuel 17:45

There are times when we need a friend, there are times when we need a provider, and there are times when we need a deliverer. In Exodus 3:14, the Lord declares that He is the "I AM." He is everything that we will ever need. Today we focus on the Lord who rules over all and who stands ready to deliver us when we feel overwhelmed by the challenges of life.

In 1 Samuel 17, the future King David finds himself standing before a seemingly overwhelming giant named Goliath. As translated in the New Living Translation, the tip of Goliath's spear alone weighed fifteen pounds (1 Samuel 17:7)—the weight of a heavy bowling ball! Imagine having the size and the strength to throw such javelin in battle! Imagine having to fight such a person! In this moment in time, the entire destiny of the nation of Israel, through whom the Messiah was to come, was in the hands of a young man whose only weapon consisted of five smooth stones which he had picked up from a brook on the way to the battlefield (1 Samuel 17:40).

When I was growing up, I spent a couple summers at the home of my grandparents, who lived in northern Minnesota. My grandpa loved to watch professional wrestling on television, and I remember the endless rhetoric between the wrestlers before each match. In the same way, in Middle Eastern culture it is common for national leaders going to battle to use exaggerated speech to strike fear in the hearts of their enemies. In the Bible, we see this in Goliath, who threatens to feed the flesh of David to the birds of the sky and the beasts of the field (1 Samuel 17:44). In response to the threats spewing forth from the mouth of Goliath, David in turn declares that he has come in the name of the Lord of Hosts, the God of the armies of Israel whom Goliath has taunted (1 Samuel 17:45).

The Hebrew name from which the Lord of Hosts is translated is *Adonai-Tsabbaoth.* There are several ways to interpret what "Hosts" may mean. First, it often refers to the myriads of angels, as in Psalm 103:20-21 and Luke 2:13. Psalm 148:1-4 not only expands "Hosts" to encompass the sun, moon and stars, but in so doing supremely exalts the Lord as the absolute highest of the highest ruler over the entire universe. The principal translation which we will focus on here is that of "armies."[146] The root verb *tsabah* means to wage war;[147] hence, David declares to Goliath that he has come in the name of the Lord over the armies. David recognizes that Goliath, as intimidating as his stature might be, has naturally superior physical strength but carries no authority. Though David finds himself physically outmatched in the natural realm, he nonetheless understands that the King of the universe has his back. In our nation the President serves as the Commander in Chief of the Armed Forces, not unlike other national leaders in their respective nations. Nevertheless, the authority that the President of the United States carries dwarfs woefully in contrast to that of the Most High God.

Several years ago when I was visiting my family in Michigan, the President came to that city to speak at a local high school. During the news broadcast, I remember seeing a young man excitedly jumping around and holding up his hand for all to see because He had just shaken hands with the most powerful man on earth. Most "common" people have little or no access to the President. Jesus, however, paid and paved the way for us to enjoy unlimited, unfettered, round-the-clock access to the Father who even knows us by name and loves us intimately. Our access to Him begins in this life and continues throughout all eternity. Hebrews 4:16 declares, "Let us therefore come boldly unto the throne of grace, that we may obtain mercy, and find grace to help in time of need."

Many of us face our own Goliaths. For some, it may be a legal battle. For others, it may be a potentially terminal illness. Still for others, it may be a financial struggle. Whatever our Goliath may look like in our personal lives, we can confidentially know that there is no struggle, no trial, nor any circumstance that surpasses the mighty power of the Almighty God. Philippians 2 boldly proclaims the following promise: "Wherefore God also hath highly exalted him, and given him a name which is above every name: That at the name of Jesus every knee should bow, of things in heaven, and things in earth, and things under the earth; and that every tongue should confess that Jesus Christ is Lord, to the glory of God the Father" (Philippians 2:9-11).

It goes without saying that trials are not enjoyable. If we had our choice, few of us would go through them. Most of us would be more than happy to live a struggle-free life where things always seem to go our way. That being said, it is the trials of life which invite the Lord Jesus to demonstrate His love and power in our individual lives. In closing, let us remember the words of the Apostle Paul as he writes the following: "And he said unto me, 'My grace is sufficient for thee: for my strength is made perfect in weakness. Most gladly therefore will I rather glory in my infirmities, that the power of Christ may rest upon me'" (2 Corinthians 12:9). *Are you facing a Goliath today? Who or what are you trusting in for your victory? Put your trust in the Lord of Hosts, and know that He will cause you to triumph in all things!*

PRAYER

Lord Jesus, I thank You that You are truly the Lord of Hosts. You are the mighty King of the universe and there is no higher name than Your most holy name. I thank You that whatever Goliaths I face, You are with me, You save me from destruction and You cause me to triumph-not only to demonstrate Your power to the world, but because You love me.

I pray this in name of Jesus!

DECLARATION

I declare that the Lord Jesus Christ is the Mighty God. He is Yahweh-Tsabbaoth, the Lord of Hosts. He rules over the angels; He rules over the sun, moon, and stars and He rules over the entire universe. Nothing will overcome me because I am in an intimate, covenant relationship with the One who rules over all creation.

I declare this by faith in Jesus' name!

QUESTIONS

1. What trials are you facing today that only the Lord of Hosts can cause you to overcome?
2. What was a time that He miraculously came through for you to deliver you from the clutches of the enemy?
3. How has your faith grown as a result of the devotional today?

DAY 28

צדק

tsadaq

He Is Our Freely-Given Righteousness

> Behold, the days come, saith the Lord, that I will raise unto David a righteous Branch, and a King shall reign and prosper, and shall execute judgment and justice in the earth. In his days Judah shall be saved, and Israel shall dwell safely: and this is his name whereby he shall be called, The Lord Our Righteousness.
> – Jeremiah 23:5-6

Many of us can recall times that we tried to become better people in some way, only to fall flat on our face within a matter of months, weeks, days, or even hours. I remember waking up after some wild parties during my high school days and vowing to never drink again, only to be right back in the same pattern that very same evening. Often we must come to the end of ourselves before we can truly understand and embrace the amazing grace of God. Through the grace of God, we are given His righteousness by faith. Today we are looking at another revealed name of God: *Adonai-Tsidqenuw*, which means, "The Lord our Righteousness."[148]

From 627 B.C to 587 B.C. the prophet Jeremiah prophesied during the final forty years before the kingdom of Judah was conquered and carried off into captivity by the Babylonian empire in 587 B.C.[149] This was the tragic conclusion to God's dealing with generation after generation of rebellion and backsliding of the very nation He had called out of the world unto Himself. The account of the Babylonian conquest of Jerusalem is narrated in 2 Kings 24-25 and 2 Chronicles 26. The Babylonian King Nebuchadnezzar initially conquered the city of Jerusalem during the reign of Jehoiachin. At this time he took away the royal family, the government officials, and all the fighting men and one thousand skilled-workers and artisans. Nebuchadnezzar then made Mattaniah, the uncle of the former King Jehoiachin, the king over the remainder of Jerusalem and Judah, and it was King Nebuchadnezzar who changed Mattaniah's name to Zedekiah (2 Kings 24:15-17), which means "Righteousness of the Lord." Here we still see the mercy of God demonstrated, in that there was still a remnant which was allowed to remain in Jerusalem. The Temple was still left standing and much of the gold, silver, and bronze articles remained untouched.

King Zedekiah ended up being a very bad king. 2 Chronicles 36:11-13 provides a sad overview of his eleven-year reign, ending with a rebellion against King Nebuchadnezzar which brought down the full wrath of the mighty Babylonian Empire down upon the city of Jerusalem. This time, city was completely decimated. The young men were slaughtered in the sanctuary and most of the remaining men and women, young and old, were taken away as captives to Babylon; the walls of the city were broken down; the Temple was destroyed and all the treasures therein were carried off; the palaces were burned down and anything left of any value was destroyed (2 Chronicles 36:17-19). The last thing King Zedekiah saw before his own eyes were put out was the brutal execution of all of his sons (2 Kings 25:7).

By virtue of the fact that King Zedekiah received his name from a Gentile king (2 Kings 24:17), the implication is that his righteousness, though in name was the righteousness of God, ultimately came from a man. Tragically, we can see from the life of King Zedekiah the fruit that his human righteousness produced. Throughout the Bible, from Genesis to Revelation, there is an ongoing war between two forms of righteousness—the righteousness which comes from man through his own human efforts and the righteousness which comes from God by faith.

Perhaps the most poignant simile of the righteousness of man is found in Isaiah 64:6, which declares, "But we are all as an unclean thing, and all our righteousnesses are as filthy rags; and we all do fade as a leaf; and our iniquities, like the wind, have taken us away." The Hebrew word for filthy is *iddah*. Herein is found the only occurrence of this word in the entire Bible and the word specifically refers to a menstrual rag.[150] While this was obviously an image of something that was physically unsanitary, it had even greater significance to the Jewish reader in that menstrual rags were considered not only physically, but ceremonially, unclean. According to the Old Testament, any woman who was having monthly period was ceremonially unclean for seven days, as well as anyone who had touched her or touched her bed, her clothing, or anything upon which she had sat. Under the Old Covenant, no person could participate in any worship to God during their period of uncleanness (Leviticus 15:19-33).

So it is with our own acts of righteousness, strived for outside of a relationship with God in a futile attempt to gain His favor.[151] Many of us have been to "white elephant" Christmas parties where we have seen worthless gifts that end up getting re-gifted from person-to-person, party-to-party, and even year-to-year. Several years ago, I went to such a party where someone had brought a half-empty box of cereal. The value of our human attempts to earn God's love and forgiveness, independent of dependence upon God, is of no more value to Him than that half-empty box of cereal. Being a good parent or employee? Box of cereal. Faithfully attending religious services? Box of cereal. Giving a fortune away to the poor? Box of cereal. Giving our life for our country or for a cause? Box of cereal. All of these things are good, but can bring us no closer to God.

So where does this leave us? Up to this point, our hope of having any righteousness may seem quite dismal, but this is where the good news comes in. Jeremiah 23:5-6 was written to the Israelites in the wake of the ruin that was King Zedekiah's reign. One commentator observes that this verse is a deliberate play on words between the implicit reference to Zedekiah (Righteousness of the Lord) and the explicit reference to *Adonai-Tsidqenuw* (The Lord is our Righteousness).[152] The man-made righteousness of Zedekiah ended in catastrophe–to himself, to his family and to his nation; but the coming righteousness that is from the Lord would be everything that

Zedekiah's feeble righteousness could never hope to be. So it is when we come to Christ by faith in what He has done through the cross—He gently takes the soiled righteousness of our human works away to the dumpster and He clothes us in the pure, glorious, splendid, unspotted righteousness of His Son, the Lord Jesus Christ. Do you remember how the Three Musketeers used to say, "All for one and one for all?" We might describe our salvation as being, "All for none and none for all." We gave Him nothing, and in exchange He gave, and continues to give, us all things (Ephesians 2:1-10)! What an amazing, loving, merciful and gracious God!

Under the Old Covenant, God demanded righteousness; but under the New Covenant, through the cross of the Lord Jesus Christ, He freely gives us His righteousness. I remember hearing evangelist Keith Wheeler speak at a graduation ceremony at Oral Roberts University. Wheeler testified of a man who, having just heard the gospel, broke down in tears. When asked why he was weeping, he replied, "This is *happy* news!" The gospel of salvation is not just "good news," it is truly *happy* news!

Tsidqenuw and *Zedekiah* (whose name would more accurately be spelled as *Tsedekiah*) are both rooted in the Hebrew word *tsadaq*, a verb meaning, "to be just, righteous."[153] Religious tradition teaches us to define righteousness by what a person does or does not do and focuses on external behavior; for example, it is said that a righteous person may go to church a lot, or that a righteous person does not drink or smoke, etc. In reality, righteousness is the full expression of goodness and the full expression of righteousness seeks out every possible opportunity to bless others. God is the fountain of all righteousness and he freely gives His righteous nature to all who come to Him by faith through His Son, the Lord Jesus Christ. Righteousness is not simple adherence to an external set of rules-it is born out of a love relationship between the Lord and us. When we are in love with Him, we desire to do what is pleasing to Him, and His righteousness naturally flows out of us. What we often do not realize is that, in the same way, the righteousness of God toward *us* is not simply rooted in His being God, but is rooted in His tender, intimate love toward each and every one of us! It is that righteousness that compelled the Father to send His Son Jesus Christ to go to the cross in our place and likewise compelled His Son Jesus Christ to gladly lay down His life for us so that we might be restored to a full relationship with Him. *Do you feel like a filthy rag? Do you want to be pure? Receive, embrace, and experience the righteousness that only He can give!*

PRAYER

Lord Jesus, I am so grateful for Your righteousness that You have freely given to me. It thank You that Your righteousness is more than a legal relationship of being declared forgiven; I thank You that it is more than simply the promise of going to heaven when I die; but above all, that Your righteousness has transformed me and continues to transform me more and more into Your image every single day.

I pray this in name of Jesus!

DECLARATION

*I declare that not only **have** the righteousness of God, but that according to 2 Corinthians 5:21, I **am** the righteousness of God in Christ Jesus. I declare that His righteousness flows from me back to God and back to others—not out of a religious sense of duty or obligation, but out of an intimate pursuit of His presence.*

I declare this by faith in Jesus' name!

QUESTIONS

1. How has your understanding of righteousness been transformed as a result of today's devotional?
2. What are some areas in your life where you have been trying to create your own righteousness? What fruit has that produced in your life?
3. What are some fruits of righteousness that Jesus has supernaturally produced in your life?

DAY 29

ברית

bᵉriyth

The Lord Alone Is Faithful to Keep His Covenant

> I will establish my covenant as an everlasting covenant
> between me and you and your descendants after you for the
> generations to come, to be your God and the God of your
> descendants after you.
> – Genesis 17:7

I used to know a coworker who lived in a covenant-controlled subdivision and was constantly in trouble with his housing association. Here are just a few of the violations he incurred: He was cited because his porch light was too bright; he was cited because he left his garage door open; he was cited for temporarily taking down part of his fence to do some work in his backyard; and he even was cited for an odd incident in which the flames in his barbecue grill got so high that it reflected in one of his upstairs windows, prompting his neighbors to call the fire department because it created the illusion that his house was on fire. For this last infraction he was subsequently fined for creating a false alarm.

God is a good God, but many of us grow up with the perception that He is anything *but* good. We are taught explicitly, implicitly, and through distortions of the experience of daily living that He is a bad God. The word that we will be highlighting today is *bᵉriyth*, which is the word used for covenant throughout the Old Testament.[154] Sadly, when we read in the Bible of the covenants which the Lord initiated at different times with His people, we liken any one of those covenants to that of the housing community described earlier. We see His covenant as one through which He continually waits for us to violate the rules so He can slam us for the slightest infractions. During my time in Air Force boot camp, I remember how we trainees were required at all times to carry a blank, folded, infraction form in our front pocket, called a "341." Each time a drill instructor or an officer walked by and spotted a violation of any of the rules, but it a uniform violation, a violation in military protocol, or whatever the case may be, they would simply demand a 341, which we were subsequently required to surrender. Accumulation of these forms led to increasing levels of punishment; hence we constantly walked around on pins and needles with the anticipation that we could be served an infraction at any time. Sadly, we see the Lord through the same lens. In so doing, our God who is truly full of mercy is instead believed to be a divine fault-finder.

Our twisted idea of His covenant becomes something like this: "If I do my best not to break the rules, then maybe I can keep from being punished by Him." Even after we have been in relationship with Christ for years, these thoughts continue to try to sneak into our minds. The theology of covenant is central throughout the whole Bible; hence, volumes and volumes have been written on this subject. It is not my intention here to go into great depth on this topic, but to marvel at the Lord's amazing grace which is demonstrated time and time again through His covenant-keeping nature.

The text today, found in Genesis 17, narrates the account of the Lord's everlasting promise to Abraham to make Him the father of many nations and to bless him and his descendents with the land of Israel. In no other chapter in the entire Bible does the word "covenant" appear more frequently—thirteen times in this chapter alone! This is a reaffirmation of a promise that God had already made with Abraham in Genesis 12 and Genesis 15. While we naturally think of covenants as being two-way legal contracts, and they often are, many of the covenants in the Bible are in fact one-sided, unconditional promises which God makes to His people-this particular covenant being a prime example of one of those promises. In the previous visitation in Genesis 15, there is a strange account of the encounter which God had with

Abraham. After God had wonderfully promised the multitude of descendents and the land to Abraham, Abraham asked, "How can *I* know that *I* will gain possession of it?" (Genesis 15:8) This was the wrong question because Abraham wanted to know how *he* was going to bring these things to pass. God wanted to make it clear that the promise was not going to be fulfilled by Abraham's human ability, but by *His* divine power alone. Rather than *tell* Abraham the answer to his question, He chose to *show* him the answer. After Abraham had brought some sacrificial animals, cut them in half and laid the halves on opposite sides of the ground, the Lord caused a deep sleep to fall on Abraham. After the sun had set, a blazing pot and a burning torch passed between the animal halves (Genesis 15:9-17). It was God alone who passed through the sacrifices. Abraham could not accompany Him because he was completely immobilized.

Clearly it was God alone who was going to bring the promises to pass without any help from Abraham. Some scholars, trying to make sense of this event, have taught that this graphic picture of the split animals was intended as a warning to the one who would break this covenant—and perhaps it was…but to whom was this warning directed? There were no conditions given to Abraham, so God could have only been only been directing such a warning to Himself if He failed to fulfill His word. Granted, in Genesis 17, God did command Abraham to be circumcised along with his household and his servants (Genesis 17:10). Even then, the circumcision was not a condition, but a sign of the covenant. In no place in the Bible is a sign ever considered to be a condition to a promise, but rather, a symbol pointing to a greater spiritual reality.

Clearly there are two-way, conditional covenants which God has established-the most obvious being the Law which was given to Moses on Mount Sinai. Even then, however, when the Israelites failed miserably to keep their end of the bargain, God did not entirely abandon them. Instead, He replaced the old external covenant which the Israelites could never hope to keep with a brand new internal covenant which *anyone* could keep. This would only be possible because they would be completely renewed and empowered by the indwelling of the Holy Spirit. This covenant would no longer be externally written in stone, but internally written in the hearts of His people (Jeremiah 31:31-33). In His mercy He chose to "dumb it down!" He made it absolutely possible for *anyone*, regardless of one's past, regardless of one's personal weaknesses or regardless of any other barriers, to be cleansed of all sin, to be fully reconciled to Him, to know Him intimately, and to enjoy Him forever as His royal sons and daughters. As we return to the Hebrew word *b^{e}riyth*, there are several theories as to how this word came about. While no theory is without flaws, each sheds a different light on what covenant means. Ultimately, the true meaning of covenant can only be determined by context.[155] That being said, we will briefly look at some of those theories here.

First, some Hebrew scholars argue that *b^{e}riyth* is rooted in the verb *barah*, which means "to eat or dine."[156] A noun form would be *biryah*, meaning "food."[157] In biblical times, covenants were sealed by the sharing of a meal. It was at the Last Supper that our Lord Jesus Christ proclaimed the New Covenant of grace which would be purchased and sealed by His own spotless blood. In Near-Eastern culture, meals were never shared with strangers—only family and friends. This custom emphasizes the foundation of relationship which was intended to undergird covenants. Covenants were not simply to be cold, legal agreements to be strictly enforced by the rule of law, but rather to be respected by a mutual understanding between two parties who held a common bond with one another.

A second argument which is most widely accepted among Hebrew experts is that the word *b^{e}riyth* finds its roots in the Akkadian word *biritu*, which means "clasp or fetter."[158] The idea of associating covenant with a bond, chain, or fetter is a metaphor, in that the strength or fastening of chains illustrates the reliability of the covenant.[159] Likewise, in the English language, we may say that one is bound to tell the truth, or bound to keep his word. A third possible source is also rooted in the Akkadian language: The Akkadian proposition *birit* means between; hence the Hebrew word *b^{e}riyth* may have evolved from the word *birit* to describe an agreement between two parties.[160]

Finally, a fourth theory states that *b^{e}riyth* is rooted in the Hebrew verb *barar*,[161] which means to "purify or select."[162] The noun form of this verb would therefore express "something (or someone) that has been specially set apart."[163] Scripture reiterates that the covenant people of God have been separated unto Him as His royal priesthood (Exodus 19:5; 1 Peter 2:9). Under the Old Covenant the Israelites were His chosen people, but under the New Covenant this privilege has been extended to all who will put their trust in Christ—whether Jew or Gentile. We as the New Testament believers have been given the ministry of reconciliation to bring a lost and dying world into a fully restored relationship with the Lord Jesus Christ (2 Corinthians 5:18-21).

All of this is purely academic unless we have entered personally into a personal *b^{e}riyth* relationship with Christ. We do so by simply entrusting our lives to Him by faith. *Have you embraced His grace and mercy? He longs to know you! He longs to lavishly pour out His love on you! Say "Yes" to Him today and watch what He will do with your life!*

PRAYER

Lord Jesus, I thank You that You made it possible for me to enter into a glorious covenant relationship with You. I acknowledge that without You I can do nothing. In the power of my own strength, I cannot possibly hope to remain faithful to any covenant with You and I cannot possibly hope to live a holy life apart from You. I give You my heart today; I give You my life today; and I surrender all that I am to You. Please take my life today and turn it into something beautiful.

I pray this in name of Jesus!

James Revoir

DECLARATION

I declare that I have entered into a covenant relationship with God the Father through His Son, the Lord Jesus Christ. It is a new and everlasting covenant, purchased by His precious blood. He empowers me to live for Him by living in Him in sweet fellowship with His Holy Spirit. He paid it all and He does it all.

I declare this by faith in Jesus' name!

QUESTIONS

1. What are some good and bad types of covenants that you see in your daily life?
2. What are some ways that the model of these good or bad covenants has strengthened or weakened your relationship with God?
3. In light of the devotional today, what does it mean to you to be in a covenant relationship with God?

DAY 30

סגלה

s*e*gullah

We Are God's One-of-a-Kind Treasure

Now therefore, if ye will obey my voice indeed, and keep my covenant, then ye shall be a peculiar treasure unto me above all people: for all the earth is mine.
– Exodus 19:5

Several years ago, I had the experience of a lifetime when I spent six months in the land of Egypt. One of the memories which remain in my mind is a brief tour of the National Archaeological Museum in Cairo which houses much of the priceless treasures of ancient Egypt. Unfortunately, our tour guide at the time spoke no English, so the best he could do was point and grunt brief phrases. Nonetheless, it was an amazing experience to be surrounded by so much gold, from small statuettes to canopies. The identity and function of many of the priceless artifacts remain a mystery, but this by no means diminishes their wonder. I am reminded that in the movie "National Treasure," there is a silent awe that comes upon the heroes when they gaze into the newly re-discovered treasure room.

When we think of the word "treasure," the picture which immediately comes to mind is that of a chest of jewels or gold coins; but this is an imperfect illustration because it still gives us a sense of sameness. I think that the treasure that God thinks of when He sees us is a vast treasure room, full of artifacts of all types, shapes, and size. Some of us are like smaller items gold and jewels, but others are more likened to larger gold statues. Treasure hunters often find things of which they have no idea as to their identity or function, but which are beautiful nonetheless. It does not matter, because the maker knew what he or she was doing. So it is with us, we may have no idea why God made us the way that He did or what He made us to be, but He knows our intrinsic value. Our job is not to figure it all out but simply to worship Him.

With the exception of coins, which can easily be sold and converted to cash, priceless treasures like works of art often have no practical value. They enrich our lives simply because of their aesthetic beauty. The world often has tendency to measure one's worth by what he or she can do. On the contrary, God values us simply because of who we are. He delights in us and rejoices over us as His precious handiwork.

When was a child, I remember going to the dentist and picking a prize out of a treasure chest if I had been good (meaning I was cooperative while my mouth was being poked and prodded). Sometimes we hear the word "treasure" and we may think that, even if we are any type of treasure, we may be worth no more than a piece of candy or plastic toy from the dollar store; but when God declares that we are His treasured possession, He is declaring that we are truly *priceless*!

When the Israelites first arrived to Mount Sinai after having been delivered by the Lord from slavery in Egypt, the Lord declared to Moses, "Now therefore, if ye will obey my voice indeed, and keep my covenant, then ye shall be a peculiar treasure unto me above all people: for all the earth is mine" (Exodus 19:5). What is truly amazing is that He reiterated that they were still His treasure after His having endured forty years of bitter complaining, strife, unbelief and the worst that the Israelites had to offer (Deuteronomy 7:6-7). How wonderful it is that the Lord never stops loving us dearly, even after we have been at our worst for years and years!

The King James Version, in its archaic language, does not do this expression justice in expressing God's vast, infinite love toward us. The Hebrew word used in Exodus 19:5 is $s^e gullah$, which means "valued property, peculiar treasure."[164] In contemporary, English versions of the Bible, the word is translated "treasured possession," which is much more endearing. This same word is used in reference to the gold, silver, bronze and jewels which King David, and later, his son King Solomon, brought and donated to the Temple (1 Chronicles

29:3; Ecclesiastes 2:8). The uniqueness and value of this treasure cannot be overstated. God owns the universe; the wealth of the nations is all His—even the wealth of Egypt and Babylon, which were two of the wealthiest empires of all time; yet above all that He owns He highly values His people as His very own treasured possession. Gold and silver and other precious metals are great, but we are His living treasures. Living beings are superior to inanimate objects.

When I was in high school, I used to think of myself as one of the faceless masses; but God takes special joy in each and every one of us because He handmade each of us (Psalm 139:13-18). When we recognize how priceless we are and how priceless others are, we naturally become more careful about how we treat others and how we treat ourselves. Have you ever handled something that was very expensive or rare? You do not throw it around carelessly, but you treat it very gently with the greatest of respect.

In Matthew 13:52, Jesus uttered a brief parable about the teachers of the Law: "He said to them, 'Therefore every teacher of the law who has been instructed about the kingdom of heaven is like the owner of a house who brings out of his storeroom new treasures as well as old.'" I think this is also a vivid picture of the amazing pride that the Father has for each and every one of us. He loves to show off His children, like a mother showing her baby pictures or a grandmother showing photos of her grandchildren. I can still remember how, when I was young, my grandparents used to have pictures of all the grandchildren proudly displayed in virtually every room in the house!

Ironically, it is said that when jewelers appraise diamonds, one of the first things they look for is a flaw. All natural diamonds have tiny flaws. Cubic zirconium diamonds are "perfect." Granted, they are phony, but they are "flawless" nonetheless. As the flaws make diamonds unique, so we all have traits that we may consider defects, but which God simply looks upon as traits that make us uniquely special. Many of us have gone through times in which we devalued our uniqueness. We have longed to change things about ourselves which we consider less than desirable. To illustrate this point, the Lord gave me a poem several years ago which expresses this frustration, but which ends in an affirmation of His never-ending love toward each and every one of us:

James Revoir

I'm Ugly

"I'm ugly!" she moaned as she looked in the mirror,
All alone in the bathroom where no one would hear her.

"My feet are too big and my thighs are too fat,
My ears are too low and my chest is too flat.

My hair is too thin and my arms are too skinny,
And what I would give to look good in a mini!"

As she stared at her image, she bitterly languished
'Til her heart broke from under the pain and the anguish.

Overwhelmed with depression, she let out a sigh;
And consumed by frustration she started to cry.

But in a moment of time, in the midst of her sadness,
Her heaviness lifted and her heart filled with gladness.

A voice that she heard from within calmed her fear,
Saying, "Daughter don't cry, but be of good cheer!

Your feet are petite and your thighs are just right;
And your ears and your chest look just fine in my sight.

Your hair is full-bodied, and your arms are not skinny;
And to be honest, I've never been a fan of the mini!

Have you not heard? Do you not understand?
That your name is engraved in the palm of my hand?
So there's no need for tears and there's no need to weep,
The beauty you have is much more than skin-deep.

And don't be dismayed by the judgments of men,
For my passionate love for you never shall end."[165]

We are truly God's treasured possession. Let's celebrate His amazing love for us!

PRAYER

Lord Jesus, I pray that You will continually open my spiritual eyes to see myself and others through Your amazing love. Please help me to see the treasure that You made me to be and please help me to build others up as I allow Your words to flow through me.

I pray this in name of Jesus!

DECLARATION

I declare that I am God's treasured handiwork. He made me special; He made me unique; He made me to be His very own one-of-a-kind possession. He takes pride in me; He rejoices over me and I bask every day in His amazing love. I was chosen by Him before the foundation of the world, so I can rest assured that His love for me will never end and that I can never undo His goodness toward me.

I declare this by faith in Jesus' name!

QUESTIONS

1. What are some of the things that make you unique as God's treasured possession?
2. If you compared yourself to a treasure, what would it be and why?
3. In what ways are you calling out the unique gifts which the Lord Jesus has placed in others?

DAY 31

דִּשֵׁן

dashen

Fatness Is in the Eye of the Beholder

> Wherefore do ye spend money for that which is not bread?
> and your labour for that which satisfieth not? Hearken
> diligently unto me, and eat ye that which is good, and let your
> soul delight itself in fatness.
> – Isaiah 55:2

When I was in college, I took an Art History class and was struck at how, in Medieval and Renaissance paintings, the idealized picture of beauty in ages past would be considered overweight and even ugly by our standards today. In more recent times, even the vintage poster women from the early twentieth century often appeared to be plump. Being fat has taken on a very bad reputation in recent generations, but this has not always been the case. Throughout most of history, fatness has been considered a symbol of prosperity when contrasted to the skinniness of the many billions of people who have lived out their entire lives in hunger and lack.

In Isaiah 55:2, through the mouth of the prophet Isaiah, the Lord invites all people to freely come to Him to enjoy the fatness of His bounty which He alone can offer. The Hebrew word for fatness is rooted in the verb *dashen*, which simply means, "to be fat or to grow fat."[166] In the Old Testament, there seems to be a special significance to fat which is not fully understood to the contemporary mind. As with blood, the Israelites were forbidden to eat the fat of the sacrifices made to Him because the fat belonged to the Lord (Leviticus 3:16-17). In contrast the modern stigma of fat being synonymous with cholesterol and hence heart disease, fat in biblical times was considered to be especially nourishing; therefore, *dashen* was associated with the idea of being satisfied, pleased, and having abundance.[167] This fatness is promised as a reward to those who are generous (Proverbs 11:25), hard-working (Proverbs 13:4), and who trust in God (Proverbs 28:25).

Too often, we associate God with stoicism and even stinginess. We think and are taught that serving Him requires that we take a vow of poverty. We come to believe that He will supply our most basic needs, but no more. In reality, our God is an abundant, generous, lavish God who longs to pour out His most wonderful blessings upon our lives. He is not the God of just enough—He is the God of more than enough! It is for this very reason that the Apostle Paul prays in Ephesians 3:20, "Now unto him that is able to do exceeding abundantly above all that we ask or think, according to the power that worketh in us."

When I was young, I used to have a grandmother who loved to spoil my two siblings and me. I remember one Christmas in particular when she came laden with three large bags full of presents—one for each of us, much to the chagrin of my parents, who made her take the gifts back to the store. In the end they did let her buy the entire family a ping-pong table. God is a good God and His goodness cannot be overstated. Unfortunately, Satan, the enemy of our souls, works overtime to make us believe that the Lord is uncaring and that He is only willing to meet our barest essential needs. *Do have any idea how much the Lord wants to lavish His most abundant blessings upon you? If you have put limits on God's lavish love for you, throw those limits off today! Believe that He will truly exceed the wildest desires of your heart!*

PRAYER

Lord Jesus, I thank you that You love me more than I can even begin to imagine. I thank You for expanding my expectation of what You can and will do in my life. You delight me with the fatness of Your blessing and I stand in awe of Your lavish love for me!

I pray this in name of Jesus!

DECLARATION

I declare that I am a royal child of God. My Father is the King of the universe who owns it all. He treats me like a prince and I have an incalculable royal inheritance. I do not need to wait for heaven to enjoy His abundance—it is available to me now! Jesus truly can and truly will bless me beyond what my mind can possibly conceive, just as the Word of God declares that He is able to do exceedingly, abundantly above all that I can possibly ask or think!

I declare this by faith in Jesus' name!

QUESTIONS

1. In what areas of your life have you had low expectations of God's abundance?
2. What is the wildest dream that you have ever had? Do you believe that God can and will meet that dream? Do you believe that He will even exceed it?
3. How has your faith been enlarged by the devotional today?

DAY 32

זית

zayith

We Are God's Olive Trees

> The Lord called thy name, A green olive tree,
> fair, and of goodly fruit.
> – Jeremiah 11:16

Remember Popeye's girlfriend, Olive Oyl?[168] With her toothpick body supported by her extremely big feet, Olive Oyl would never have been mistaken for being a supermodel; nevertheless she held a special place in Popeye's heart. In the devotional today, we will see why she is so aptly named as we compare the love between Popeye and Olive Oyl to our own relationship with God.

The Hebrew word which we will be exploring today is *zayith*. Depending on the context, it is used interchangeably throughout the Old Testament in reference to either olives or olive trees.[169] *Zayith* is a common word, occurring thirty-eight times in the Old Testament.[170] In modern times, olives have been more or less relegated to an aisle in the grocery store. In biblical times, however, the fruit of olive trees was such that olives touched every aspect of daily living. Commentators find it noteworthy that, based on one single leaf, Noah recognized the olive branch which the dove brought back to him in Genesis 8:11. This bears witness to the importance of the olive tree in even the earliest of times. Following are some of the common uses of olives, olive trees, and olive oil in biblical times:

- Olives were eaten and olive oil was used in cooking.
- Olive wood was used for carpentry and woodwork.[171]
- Olive oil, because of its healing power, was used to anoint kings as a way of promoting their health.[172]
- Olive oil was used for purification.[173]
- Olive oil was used as fuel for lamps (Matthew 25:1-13).[174]

One would expect that such an important tree would be tall and stately, but in reality the olive tree is known for its fat, gnarled appearance. The prophet Isaiah, in describing the first coming of the Messiah, makes a veiled comparison of the Lord Jesus Christ to the olive tree: "For he shall grow up before him as a tender plant, and as a root out of a dry ground: he hath no form nor comeliness; and when we shall see him, there is no beauty that we should desire him" (Isaiah 53:2). Likewise, we as His believers, do not always measure up to the standards of beauty and eloquence as defined by the world system; nevertheless, when we walk in union with Him, our lives bear much fruit by the power of the Holy Spirit (1 Corinthians 2:1-5).

Olive trees do not require much water.[175] Too often, we as believers buy into the lie that the fruit that we bear is limited by our present circumstances. We look at the things we seem to lack in our lives and look to the day when conditions will be more ideal-*then* we will bear fruit. The paradox of the Christian life is that, throughout history, the greatest revivals have often come under times of tremendous persecution. We see this occurring from the New Testament church of the first century to the modern, exponential growth of the underground church in China.

Olive trees are similar to weeds, in that they cannot be killed by simply cutting them down, for their roots will simply sprout up brand new shoots. In the same way, each time the enemy has tried throughout history to destroy the church through persecution, the church has only multiplied. We see this played out in the Book of Acts when the Church is scattered by affliction and ends up growing and flourishing wherever the people of God flee. The enemy is frequently at work in our lives, trying to crush and destroy us; but each time we turn our eyes upon the Lord Jesus Christ, He multiplies new victories in our lives in areas that we would have never dreamed of on our own. I experienced this personally in 2008, when, after graduating from Oral Roberts University, I moved down to Texas with the intention of receiving further ministerial training. Unfortunately, I moved ahead of the will of God for my life at that time and in the process I lost everything. I totaled my truck, I had no job, I had no money, and I was living week-to-week in a transient motel. At the end of four months of unsuccessful job searching, I limped back to Denver, which had been my home for many years prior to Oral Roberts University. Upon my return, some wonderful friends took me into their home, rent-free, while I looked for a job. In the process, I came into an amazing church fellowship, through which I was introduced to a truly intimate relationship with Jesus, on a deeper level than I had ever known in my life. As a result, I began to sprout fruit in areas of my life that I had never before imagined possible.

Olive trees are commonly known to live for centuries. Some have been reported to be two thousand years or older and still producing. On the Mount of Olives in Jerusalem, next to the Church of All Nations which is built over the rock upon which the Lord Jesus Christ is said to have poured out His heart on the night of His arrest, there is a grove of olive trees called "The Silent Witnesses." This grove is so-called because the olive trees are said to have been alive when Christ prayed in the garden.

Like the longevity of the olive tree which lives long after the one who planted and tended it has passed on and has been forgotten, it is God's intention that we bear fruit which remains long after we are gone. Jesus said, "Ye have not chosen me, but I have chosen you, and ordained you, that ye should go and bring forth fruit, and that your fruit should remain: that whatsoever ye shall ask of the Father in my name, he may give it you" (John 15:16). I am a believer today because of the witness of a high school friend who went on to be with the Lord in 1994. I believe that wonderful, departed friend of mine continues to receive a heavenly commission payment on all the good fruit that I bear—even after he has gone from this world.

God has planted destiny in the hearts of every believer and that destiny transcends the struggles of daily life which constantly clamor for our attention. The moment we yield our lives to the Lord Jesus Christ, He gives us the gift of His Holy Spirit who comes to live within us. Throughout the Scripture, olive oil represents the power and the anointing of the Holy Spirit. As we walk in union with the Holy Spirit day-by-day, all of the physical attributes of the olive and the olive tree which we have discussed today will become a spiritual reality in our lives; that is, we will be a constant source of refreshing to others, we will bear much wonderful fruit and that fruit will remain long after we are gone. *Do you truly know Jesus? Are you truly experiencing the abundance of His Holy Spirit in your life? If you are not sure, let Him plant His olive tree in your heart today, and watch what He will produce in you!*

PRAYER

Lord Jesus, I thank You that You have sent Your wonderful Holy Spirit to live in me. I pray that I will not be satisfied with simply surviving this life, but that my life will bear an abundance of fruit each and every day. Please fill me to overflowing with Your presence and Your power.

I pray this in name of Jesus!

DECLARATION

I declare that I am a child of God. Because I am His child, His Holy Spirit lives in me without measure. Like healthy olive tree, my life refreshes others, my life bears much fruit and that fruit remains! My heart and my being overflows with the love, the power, the presence, and the anointing of the Holy Spirit toward every person whom I encounter.

I declare this by faith in Jesus' name!

QUESTIONS

1. In light of what you have learned about olives and olive trees, what fruit has the Holy Spirit produced in your life?
2. What kind of fruit do you believe that the Holy Spirit desires to produce in you, which you perhaps not yet experienced?
3. How do we cultivate the anointing of the Holy Spirit in our lives?

DAY 33

רמש

remes

Creepy, Crawly Things

> So I went in and saw; and behold every form of creeping things, and abominable beasts, and all the idols of the house of Israel, portrayed upon the wall round about.
> – Ezekiel 8:10

Many of us have a natural fear of or repulsion toward snakes and spiders. My father has always had an infamous fear of snakes. One time when I was growing up, my sister put a rubber snake in a ceramic pitcher just before he picked it up. When he saw the snake in the pitcher, he threw it across the garage and smashed it into a million pieces. The eighth chapter of the Book of Ezekiel gives account of creepy, crawler critters being secretly worshipped in the holy Temple of the Lord. We will see today that when people do not have a relationship with God, they will go to extreme measures to find someone or something else to desperately fill that void.

Ezekiel was a prophet who ministered during a very dark period in the history of Israel. After generations of backsliding and rebellion against the Lord, the glorious city of Jerusalem was invaded and burned to the ground and its surviving inhabitants were carried off into captivity to Babylon by King Nebuchadnezzar. This happened in three stages:[176] First, Nebuchadnezzar besieged the city during the reign of King Jehoiakim in 605 B.C. (2 Kings 24:1). At this time, he took away the cream of the crop of the Israelites, including Daniel and his friends Hananiah, Mishael, and Azariah, better known as Shadrach, Meshach, and Abednego (Daniel 1:1-7). The second stage occurred in 597 B.C. during the reign of King Jehoiachin, son of Jehoiakim, who began to reign after his father's death. At this time, Nebuchanezzar laid siege to the city again, took away the treasures of the Temple and the royal palace, and carried off ten thousand captives, leaving behind only the poorest people in the land (2 Kings 24:8-16). It was during this second siege that Ezekiel was taken away.[177] The third and final blow came in 586 B.C. when the puppet king, Zedekiah, installed by Nebuchanezzar, led a rebellion which brought down the full wrath of the mighty Babylonian army. This time the Temple, the royal palaces and all the other great homes of the city were burned to the ground. The walls around Jerusalem were broken down and almost all the remaining inhabitants were taken to Babylon (2 Kings 25:1-11).

Around 592 B.C., the Lord appeared to Ezekiel in Babylon and in a vision, picked him up by his hair and carried him back to Jerusalem (Ezekiel 8:2-3). At this time, the Temple was still standing, albeit plundered, and there were still inhabitants living in Jerusalem who had not yet been carried off. During this vision, the Lord showed him seventy elders who were secretly worshipping the images of all kinds of bugs and beasts and other idols, deep inside the Temple: "So I went in and saw; and behold every form of creeping things, and abominable beasts, and all the idols of the house of Israel, portrayed upon the wall round about" (Ezekiel 8:10).

The Hebrew word for "creeping things" is *remes*. This word speaks of things that move around on the ground.[178] In Psalm 104:20, the same word is used of animals that prowl around in the night. Furthermore, Ezekiel 8:10 adds that the elders were also giving homage to "abominable beasts." The Hebrew word for abominable, *shiqqutz*, describes those things which are absolutely detestable.[179] When I was a child, I remember a time when my mother had made a large bowl of rice pudding and had put it outside to cool but forgot about it until it was discovered a couple weeks later, infested with maggots. Being the boy in the family, I was tasked with cleaning out the bowl. To this day, I consider that experience with the rotting stench, the thousands of slithering, writhing larvae and the buzzing flies to be the most repulsive experience of my entire life. I kept

Priceless Stones

walking away from the scene because I was continually being overwhelmed by an involuntary, gag reflex.

Many of us in the Christianized West know that the first command of the Ten Commandments states that we are to have no other gods before the Lord our God (Exodus 19:3). While we would not consider physically prostrating ourselves before an idol—especially an idol of a bug or a snake-the reality is that when we make anything on this earth more powerful than God, we are in fact ascribing worship to that earthly thing. When we are going through the trials of life and we choose to walk in fear, we are in effect worshipping our circumstances over God.

It goes without saying that the greatest tests of our faith come during times of calamity. During these times in our lives, we are often quick to run after everything *except* God. In the account in the eighth chapter of Ezekiel, there were seventy men in individual "cubicles," each of whom was burning incense to his own, favorite god. So it is in our lives when we face trials and tribulations—perhaps we do not overtly worship idols of wood, gold or silver, but during these hard times we are often quick to run after other things that bring us temporal comfort or provide some semblance of human security, rather than running to the One who is beckoning us to come and find our rest in Him alone. We may run to our friends. We may run to the refrigerator. We may run to television. We may run to our computer. We may run to cigarettes. We may run to drugs or alcohol. We may run to music. We may run to our jobs. We may run to the mall. We may run to our bank accounts or our credit cards. We may even run to religion. Any one of these things, even those that seem good on the surface, can become idols when we exalt them above God.

The greatest moments of temptation to turn away from God toward other idols often come when we feel like we have been forsaken by Him. So it was with the idolatrous worshippers in the Temple who justified their actions in their hearts by telling themselves, "The Lord seeth us not, the Lord hath forsaken His land" (Ezekiel 8:12). One writer observes that in so declaring, they were blaming God for their rebellion.[180] Rather than blaming God for our unbelief, we would do well to follow the example of the Lord Jesus Christ. At the cross of

Calvary, the darkest moment in human history, even Christ felt abandoned by His heavenly Father to the point of crying out, "My God, My God, why hast Thou forsaken Me?" (Psalm 22:1; Matthew 27:46). This was in fulfillment of a messianic prophecy found in Psalm 22; yet the psalmist, foreseeing the attitude of Christ, triumphantly declares of Him, "I will declare thy name unto my brethren: in the midst of the congregation will I praise thee" (Psalm 22:22).

One final observation about this account is the fact that the idol worshippers were not off in the high places where they were normally to be found, but right in the Temple, albeit in secrecy. The temptation to run to other gods in difficult times is certainly not limited to the world which does not know God, but can secretly be just as real a struggle for our brothers and sisters in the body of Christ—even within our own churches. Rather than condemning them for their unbelief, which unfortunately is not uncommon, the greater act of love is to build them up in their moments or seasons of weakness. Along these same lines, King Solomon wrote the following exhortation: "Two are better than one; because they have a good reward for their labour. For if they fall, the one will lift up his fellow: but woe to him that is alone when he falleth; for he hath not another to help him up" (Ecclesiastes 4:9-10).

When I was a student at Oral Roberts University, one of the highlights each year was the annual seminary retreat. I will never forget the last retreat that I attended. After a Friday evening service, the plan was to gather around a campfire for a time of testimony and worship. Being in a wilderness area, the path to the fire pit was pitch-black. As my friends and I were walking along the trail to the fire pit, there arose a commotion from the people at the front of the line. When the rest of us caught up to them, we found that the path to the fire pit was crisscrossed by spider webs, and hanging from the trees were some of the biggest spiders that I had ever seen! Their fat, ugly bodies alone were about one and a half inches in diameter. Since it was well after dark, the only way we could see them was by flashlights that some of the students were shining on them, and there was an unspoken fear that there were even more unseen spiders lurking in the dark. Almost of the students-all of which were grown adults-were absolutely paralyzed with fear of going any further and many had decided to forego the campfire for fear of walking through one of the spider webs or having a spider fall on them. It was then that an amazing thing happened—a spirit of boldness came upon some of the braver students who offered to go ahead of everyone else and escort the more fearful students. Eventually, every one of the students walked the gauntlet of "Spider Hollow," and what began as a fearful experience ended up being a wonderfully unifying time of bonding.

When we see others who are struggling with fear and confusion because their circumstances seem to have been temporarily exalted above the power of God, it is pleasing to the Lord Jesus Christ when we build one another up in faith. Through our intercession, our prayers of agreement, and our words of life, we can walk others through these valleys and their confidence in the one true God and in His Almighty power can not only be restored, but taken to higher levels than ever before! *Who are you escorting through the spider webs of life? Ask the Lord to show you those whom you might embolden to overcome fear, and watch how He will use you in a mighty way to walk them through to victory!*

PRAYER

Lord Jesus, I thank You that You help me to keep my eyes, my mind, my heart, and my whole being focused on You and You alone. When hard times come my way, I choose not to turn to anyone or anything but You. I thank You that You are so much bigger than any of the trials or tribulations that I may encounter in my life. Your name is higher and greater than the worst that life can throw my way, and I thank You that by Your grace and Your Spirit in me, I will never let anything ever remove You from Your rightful throne.

I pray this in name of Jesus!

DECLARATION

I declare that the Lord Jesus Christ is bigger than any of my problems. His name is higher than any other name. I will not pay homage to my problems by making them more powerful than my God. When trials come, I remain steadfast and keep my mind and my heart focused on Him and Him alone. I do not run to worldly comforts or rely on worldly solutions, but I find all of my comfort and all of the answers to my problems through the comfort and wisdom of the Holy Spirit who lives in me.

I declare this by faith in Jesus' name!

QUESTIONS

1. Have you ever gone through a trial that sent you into a tailspin of fear or confusion? When it was all said and done, did your worst fear come to pass?
2. Recall a time when you trusted in God to take you through a trial. What was the outcome?
3. Who are some people in your life who are going through difficult times right now? How can you walk alongside them to point them to the God?

DAY 34

רפה

raphah

Never Left, Never Forsaken

There shall not any man be able to stand before thee all the
days of thy life: as I was with Moses, so I will be with thee: I
will not fail thee, nor forsake thee.
– Joshua 1:5

Many of us have known the experience of being stood up by someone or forgotten. I remember a time when I was in high school back in the days of my youth in Michigan. My cousin had promised to take me to a Pistons game in the Pontiac Silverdome but never showed up. What a lonely feeling to be standing by the window, waiting for someone who never bothered to come. Some of us, if we dare to admit it, have felt like there have been times when we have been stood up by God. It has been my experience that much resistance to the gospel and to the Kingdom is not rooted in theological issues, but in pivotal events in people's lives in which God did not move in the way that they had hoped. The events left them disappointed, angry and bitter. The question often arises, "Where was God when...?"

We can not always understand the ways of God (Isaiah 55:8-9), but we can know that He is always a good God and that He truly works all things together for those who love Him (Romans 8:28). The Scripture today, Joshua 1:5, is an exhortation which was given to Joshua, the newly promoted leader who had been chosen by God to lead the Israelites into the Promised Land after the death of Moses. Joshua was not one who was normally given to being fearful. After all, it was only

Caleb and he who had been willing to trust God when the twelve spies initially went in shortly after the Exodus to spy out the Promised Land (Numbers 14:6-9). The bold faith of Joshua and Caleb so incensed the Israelites that they sought to stone both of them (Numbers 14:10). Forty years later, the Lord was assuring Joshua of His power and presence as Joshua faced the daunting task of leading the entire nation by faith into the land which God had promised in previous generations to Abraham, Isaac, and Jacob. If ever there was a time when Joshua needed to be assured of the presence of the Lord, it was then, and God, being well aware of the many butterflies in Joshua's stomach, came to promise him that He would be with him and that He would not forsake him when he needed Him most.

Joshua 1:5 contained three wonderful promises—the first promise was something that the Lord *would* do and other two promises were things that He *would not* do. First of all, the Lord promised Joshua that, just as He had been with Moses, He would be with Joshua. This was no small thing to Joshua. The Lord was not simply promising a passive, powerless, feel-good presence in the background of Joshua's life. Unfortunately, when we speak of the presence of God, such a life is what we are often quick to assume. Think of all the amazing signs and wonders that the Lord did through Moses...These wonders include the ten plagues, the parting of the Red Sea, the military victories and all the healings and miraculous provisions in the wilderness over the course of forty years. The Lord was now promising that this very same power was now going to be demonstrated through the life of Joshua, and indeed it was.

As wonderful as the promise of God's presence was to Joshua, we as New Covenant believers have an even greater promise! Under the Old Covenant, the Holy Spirit would occasionally come upon certain people for a specific purpose and then leave. Under the New Covenant, the Holy Spirit no longer simply comes upon us for a short time—He comes to dwell in us forever; hence the promise in Hebrews 13:5 is that He will never leave us nor forsake us. What is even greater is that, because of the permanent indwelling of the Holy Spirit, Jesus promised that we as His children by faith would do even greater works than He did during His earthly ministry. In John 14:12, the Lord Jesus Christ made this astounding promise to His disciples: "Verily, verily, I say unto you, He that believeth on me, the works that I do shall he do also; and greater works than these shall he do; because I go unto my Father." This is no less true for us today. Jesus opened the eyes of the blind-we will do greater works. Jesus opened the ears of the deaf—we will do greater works. Jesus cast out demons—we will do greater works. Jesus made the lame to walk—we will do greater works. Jesus even raised the dead—and still, we will do even greater works!

Having promised to Joshua what He *was* going do, the Lord went on to declare what He *was not* going to do-He would never fail Joshua and He would never forsake him. The first verb translated "fail" comes from the Hebrew word *raphah*, which literally means "to sink or relax."[181] The second Hebrew word used here is *azab*, meaning "to leave, abandon, or forsake."[182] The same word is used of armies abandoning their posts in fear in times of battle (1 Samuel 31:7; 1 Chronicles 10:7; 2 Kings 7:7). In the New Testament, the same promise is reiterated to us as believers in the Lord Jesus Christ (Hebrews 13:5). In this verse, the writer emphatically reminds us that He has promised that He will never leave us; He will never forsake us. What is lost in translation is that the original Greek grammatically construction uses the expression *ou me* which is the strongest negative expression possible. Not only does it mean "never," but it is even better translated "never ever!" and communicates the idea that the very thought of His forsaking or abandoning us is absolutely unthinkable!

I can remember a period of time when I struggled with feeling abandoned by God. After I graduated from Oral Roberts University in 2008, I moved to Dallas, Texas for further schooling. No sooner had I moved down there than it seems that my life fell completely apart. First, I totaled my truck; then the plans that I had for financing the schooling did not work out, so I had to withdraw from the school and find a job. A job search which I had expected to complete within a couple weeks turned into a four month ordeal, during which time I was living in a transient motel and surviving on credit cards. At the very same time, there was a massive stock market crash and the economy plummeted.

So there I was, all alone in a strange city with no job, no vehicle, no home and no money. If ever there was a time that I felt forsaken by God, it was then. As stated earlier, Jesus declares in Hebrews 13:5, "I will never leave thee, nor forsake thee." Be that as it may, because of my circumstances at that time I found myself beginning to doubt His faithfulness and wondering what that could *really* mean. In time He proved that He means *exactly* what He says! Sometimes the Lord does not always respond to our prayers in the way we expect or even desire, but we can always rest assured that He is always in control and always works things to a greater good than we can possible imagine on our own. In spite of my disappointment and frustration at the time, I never succumbed to the temptation to abandon my relationship with Him. When I had completely come to the end of myself, He led me back to Denver. On my first day back, a friend at church handed me five hundred dollars, and then some dear old friends took me into their home free of charge while I was searching for work, a process which still took another six months. Above all, the Lord led me into an amazing body of believers, and it is through this church that I was introduced to a new level of Kingdom living which I had never known. To this day, I still remember walking under the hot Dallas sun to my motel room, crying out to God that I wanted my life back. In His love and wisdom, He did not give my life back—instead He gave me so much more!

It is vitally important to understand that all the promises made to Joshua were made on a personal level. In the Hebrew, each reference to "you" is made in the second person, masculine, singular form. While the promises certainly pertained to the nation of Israel as a whole, they were delivered on a one-on-one level to Joshua. Too often when we read the Bible, we readily understand that the promises are certainly true to the people of God on a mass, corporate level, but we often lose sight of the fact that the Lord is concerned about each and every one of us on an intimate, personal level. Jesus loves the world, but true faith is ignited when we have a revelation that Jesus loves us individually with a passion that we cannot even begin to comprehend. So it is that He has the very hairs of our heads numbered (Matthew 10:30). *Do you truly believe that He is with you and that He will never leave you nor forsake you? If you are not sure, ask Him to reveal Himself to you and get ready to watch Him do amazing things in your life!*

PRAYER

Lord Jesus, I pray that You are revealing Your presence in my life. Show me those times in the past that You have been with me when I have not readily seen Your hand. Show me how You are working in my life today and show me how You are working in the lives of others so that I may speak encouragement to those who are feeling hopelessness and despair.

I pray this in name of Jesus!

DECLARATION

I declare that the Lord Jesus Christ is always with me wherever I go. He will never leave me and He will never forsake me. He loves me passionately and desires to display His glory in and through me. He is with me because His Holy Spirit lives inside of me. When I am overwhelmed by the circumstances of life, I choose to call to remembrance the promise that "Greater is He that is in me than he that is in the world" (1 John 4:4).

I declare this by faith in Jesus' name!

QUESTIONS

1. How do you sense the presence of God in your current circumstances?
2. In what miraculous ways has the Lord been with you in the past?
3. If you are uncertain that the Lord is truly with you, what would it take to show you that He truly is working in your life? Have you asked Him?

DAY 35

הלל

halal

How to Out-Shine the Frogs and the Crickets

> Let every thing that hath breath praise the Lord.
> Praise ye the Lord.
> – Psalm 150:6

Several years ago in Oklahoma, I stopped at a rest area late at night and stepped out of my vehicle to the cacophony of hundreds tiny, hidden critters, all happily chirping and squawking away. As I wondered what so many bugs could possibly have to talk about, Psalm 150:6 came to my mind, which declares, "Let every thing that hath breath praise the Lord." It was then that I became thoroughly convinced that these creatures were not merely speaking to one another, but that they were praising the Lord with their little mouths and bodies. How truly sad it is that we, the crown jewel of creation who have been made in the image of God with the expressed purpose of worshipping Him, should be outdone by a bunch of frogs and crickets!

Psalm 150 ends the Book of Psalms with a bang! It is the culminating crescendo of the entire anthology, intended to be no less magnificent than the final movements of "Handel's Messiah" or the "1812 Overture." It is no less dramatic than the grand finale of a Fourth of July fireworks display over the Statue of Liberty. By this point in the Book of Psalms, we have experienced every range of emotion with the psalmists, almost as if we have personally accompanied them on an epic journey of faith. In this brief poem of only six verses, the command to praise the Lord appears no less than thirteen times-three times in verse one alone and twice in each subsequent verse. The primary Hebrew command to *halal* should not be unfamiliar to us-it is the root verb found in *Hallelujah* which is universally recognized to mean, "Praise the Lord!" The primary meaning of the verb *halal* is "to shine."[183] The very same word also means "to be boastful or to praise."[184] It is no coincidence that the sixth stanza of John Newton's timeless hymn "Amazing Grace" expresses how our praises to God causes us to shine with His glory:

> When we've been here ten thousand years
> Bright shining as the sun.
> We've no less days to sing God's praise
> Than when we've first begun.[185]

In our Western culture, we have been conditioned to be emotionally reserved in our thanksgiving to God and we tend to keep such emotions confined in our hearts. True praise, however, is meant to be loud and exuberant! To praise the Lord is to exult Him and to boast in Him.[186] In the ancient Akkadian language, the same word meant "to shout, to acclaim, to rejoice."[187] In that same culture, the interjection *alalu!* was a shout or song cried out by excited laborers.[188] In modern Arabic, the cognate *halla* means, "to sing joyfully to someone" and *tahalla* expresses the idea of "shouting with joy."[189]

The biblical writer Job declares that the very breath that we have comes directly from God, observing, "If he set his heart upon man, if he gather unto himself his spirit and his breath; All flesh shall perish together, and man shall turn again unto dust" (Job 24:14-15). That being the case, one modern writer comes to the conclusion that it is fitting that we praise the Lord with the very breath that He has given to us: "The breath of life is, in the long last the human being's only possession, and in this the human being is dependent upon the Lord (Isaiah 2:22). No other use of breath could be more right and true to life than praise of the Lord."[190]

When we set our minds to meditating upon who He is and all that He has done for us, we cannot help but be overwhelmed with jubilant praise! *If you do not have a revelation of Him that sends you an excitement overdrive, ask Him to show you these things! He is an amazing God! He is an awesome God! And He is more than worthy of all our praise! So the next time you hear the crickets chirping outside your window at night, do not tell them to shut up! Join in their praises to our mighty, glorious, magnificent God!*

PRAYER

Lord Jesus, I ask You to open my eyes to all that You have done for me. Show me the depth of Your love to such a degree that I cannot help but pour out my praises to You—in my thoughts, in my words, and in everything that is in me! Let the words of my mouth be a delightful outpouring of thanksgiving unto You always and everywhere!

I pray this in name of Jesus!

DECLARATION

I declare that I am a lover of God. I choose to praise Him at all times, not as a means of flattery or because I have an agenda, but simply for who He is, what He has done in my life, what He is doing, and what He has yet to do. I will not be silenced; I will not be ashamed, but I will exuberantly pour out my heart to Him, the fruit of my lips giving praise.

I declare this by faith in Jesus' name!

QUESTIONS

1. How often do you delight yourself in the Lord?
2. What do you have to praise Him for today?
3. When was the last time you excitedly overflowed with praise to Him? How about taking a moment to praise Him right now?

DAY 36

קנא

qana

He Loves Us with a Passionate Jealousy

For thou shalt worship no other god: for the Lord,
whose name is Jealous, is a jealous God.
– Exodus 34:14

Contrary to the common misperception that God sits in the heavens and has little personal involvement in our lives, He is in fact a God who passionately loves each and every one of us with a fervent love that we can not even begin to comprehend, and there are several instances in the Old Testament Scriptures in which He unashamedly reveals Himself as a jealous God, to such an extent that He even identifies His name as Jealous in Exodus 34:14.

The Hebrew adjective for jealous is *qanna*,[191] the adjective form of the verb *qana*, which means "to be jealous or zealous."[192] Linguistic scholars believe that the verb *qana* was originally rooted in an ancient verb which meant "to become intensely red." Because our face often tends to change color when we experience intense emotions, it was natural that this primitive word should eventually evolve into a modern usage to express anger, zeal, or jealousy.[193] To this day, a similar, modern Arabic word is translated, "to become intensely red (or black) with dye."[194] In the Bible, the Hebrew adjective *qanna* is an intensely passionate word used only in reference to God, which expresses His burning desire to have an exclusive relationship with each of us, undiluted by any straying devotion to any other form of a god which would diminish our love toward Him.

There are some who might take offense that a perfect God can be capable of jealousy, but it is noteworthy that the adjective *qanna* is always used only with reference to God and never to man.[195] It is therefore not justifiable to reduce God to the level of fallen humanity. In the Bible, jealousy is often associated with the marital covenant.[196] Our relationship with our Lord is no longer one of master and servant; nor is it simply a relationship between friends. To the contrary, when we come into relationship with God through the Lord Jesus Christ, we enter into nothing less than a marital covenant with Him. In the Old Testament, the Lord was described as the husband of Israel (Isaiah 54:5; Isaiah 62:5; Hosea 2:19). In the New Testament, the Church is described as the bride of Christ (Ephesians 5:25-33; Revelation 21:2, 9; Revelation 22:17). This is not just figurative language! When we receive Christ, we quite literally became His bride and we truly become one flesh with Him. The Apostle Paul says of this union, "This is a profound mystery" (Ephesians 5:32). With all of his direct, divine revelation, even Paul could not fully fathom this with his human mind. Rather than accusing or implying that the Lord is petty because of His jealousy for us, ought we not to *marvel* that the God and Creator of the universe loves each of us so passionately and intimately that His heart is broken when we stray from Him? *How can we continue to feel worthless and insignificant when we truly understand His amazing passion toward us? With this understanding, receive His love; embrace His love; and know in your heart that you are truly precious and priceless in His sight!*

PRAYER

Lord Jesus, I stand in awe of You that You consider me worthy to be called Your bride. Help me to walk in the reality of this revelation every moment of every day, and let the truth of this exude my every thought, word, and deed. I love You with all of my heart and I give myself wholeheartedly to You and You alone.

I pray this in name of Jesus!

DECLARATION

I declare that I am the bride of Christ. He gave Himself for Me and purchased Me with His own precious blood so that I might be called His very own. He loves me and treasures me more than I can possibly imagine. By the power of His Holy Spirit who lives in Me, I vow to remain faithful to Him and Him alone. I will not wander and I will not stray, but I will keep my heart pure and focused on Him. He is my God, He is my King, He is my husband and He is my eternal lover.

I declare this by faith in Jesus' name!

QUESTIONS

1. When you meditate upon the truth that Jesus loves you so much that He becomes jealous over you, what does that do to your faith?
2. How does your identity as the bride of Christ affect your walk with Him?
3. Many believers continue to see themselves as nothing more than "sinners saved by grace." Although this is certainly true, do you believe that God wants us to continue to dwell upon this identity after we have been born again? Why or why not?

DAY 37

זרק

zaraq

We Are Clean, Shiny and Pure!

> Then will I sprinkle clean water upon you, and ye shall be clean: from all your filthiness, and from all your idols, will I cleanse you. A new heart also will I give you, and a new spirit will I put within you: and I will take away the stony heart out of your flesh, and I will give you an heart of flesh.
> – Ezekiel 36:25-26

What a glorious feeling it is to be clean, especially after having become totally filthy! I remember a time many years ago when I was stationed in the Middle East and a group of us had gone snorkeling in the Red Sea. Although the day had been amazingly unforgettable, the ride back to the base was painfully irritating. I remember the salt on my sunburned legs rubbing against the hot, vinyl seats of the old school bus and wanting nothing more than to jump in the shower and to be refreshed with a cold drink as soon as I got back to my living quarters. Unfortunately, being stationed in the middle of the desert, my fellow airmen and I often had to deal with the inconvenience of water shortages. It turned out that this was one of those very days. I remember turning on the water in the shower to find that nothing was coming out of the shower head! It was then that I learned that all of the water throughout the entire installation had been turned off due to rationing. After some time and a lot of complaining, the water was restored and I enjoyed one of the best shower experiences that I have ever had in my life!

Even more wonderful than being *physically* clean is to be *spiritually* clean! The opportunity to be spiritually clean of all sin and all unrighteousness has been freely and generously extended to all who will put their faith in the Lord Jesus Christ, who, when He went to the cross, paid for all the sins of every single person who ever has lived and ever will live. In Isaiah 1:18, the Lord beckons us, "Come now, and let us reason together, saith the Lord: though your sins be as scarlet, they shall be as white as snow; though they be red like crimson, they shall be as wool."

When I was growing up, I spent a couple summers at the home of my grandparents in northern Minnesota. My grandfather lived on a wooded lot, so we spent many days doing heavy work around the property. This work ranged from building to moving to cutting down trees and removing stumps. Each day would end with a long, hot bath which would leave a filthy ring of filth in the tub. In the same way, when we come to Christ, He takes the most heinous of our sin and restores our innocence to that of a newborn babe. Over the course of a lifetime, we can accumulate enough sin and filth to fill several Olympic-sized swimming pools-not only with plain old dirt and mud, but with tar, bloodstains, and toxic waste. Nevertheless, there is no sin too great and no lifestyle so depraved that it cannot be completely cleansed by the blood that Jesus shed on the cross of Calvary.

In Ezekiel 36:25, the Lord promised that He was going to sprinkle clean water upon His people, the wayward Israelites, and that they would then be clean. The Hebrew word used in this verse is *zaraq*. This is a ceremonial word which is used specifically of water in this passage only. In most other instances in the Old Testament, *zaraq* is associated exclusively with the sprinkling of blood.[197] Under the sacrificial system, the priests were commanded to sprinkle the blood of the slain animals upon the altar. In our modern English language, when we hear the word "sprinkle" we naturally think in terms of flicking tiny droplets, but the literal meaning of *zaraq* means "to toss or to throw (in a volume)" or "to scatter abundantly."[198] The normal Hebrew word in the original biblical text which is used with the sprinkling of water, though not used in this verse, is *nazah*. The verb *nazah* means "to spurt, spatter, or sprinkle."[199] *Nazah,* used with both water and blood, often described how people such as the priests (Numbers 8:7) and objects such as houses (Leviticus 14:51) were to be cleansed from uncleanness and defilement. It would seem at first glance that the Lord is mixing metaphors in Ezekiel 36:25, but the point being made is that true spiritual cleansing was inseparable from the sprinkling of the blood from the sacrifice.[200]

The resulting promise of the sprinkling of the water was that Israel would be clean. The Hebrew verb used for clean is *taher*. This word goes beyond describing one who has been externally washed, and even beyond one who has had his sins removed. *Taher* literally means "to be clean or pure."[201] Hence, it speaks of one who has been made absolutely pure in the sight of the Most Holy God. In Malachi 3:3, the same word is used of pure, refined gold and silver which has been purified of all dross. Moreover, in Job 37:21, the same word is used to describe an absolutely cloudless sky on a gorgeous, sunny day. In the building of the tabernacle in the wilderness, the Lord commanded Moses that the instruments to be made for use by the priests were to be made of "pure gold" (*zahab tahor*) (Exodus 25, Exodus 30:3).[202] Exodus 24:10 describes how Moses, Aaron and the elders of Israel went up to Mount Sinai and saw the throne of God. In this verse, the word *tahor* is used to describe the gleaming, shiny quality of the sapphire pavement under the feet of the Lord.[203]

When the Lord purifies us, He does not simply clean us up on the outside—He purifies us on the inside of all defects. To illustrate this promise in modern terms, it is common for people to purchase a brand new vehicle—perhaps one that has just come off the assembly line—which appears to be shiny and new on the outside but ends up being an absolute lemon! God does not create lemons nor does he transform us into lemons. He makes us shiny and new on the outside and completely free from defects on the inside.

As wonderful as it is to be cleansed and purified, cleansing and purification alone as a one-time event cannot sustain us in the long run to live a holy life. We must be supernaturally empowered to overcome sin and temptation, and that power can only come from God. When I was in middle school, I as a Catholic at the time participated one evening in the sacrament of Confession. As scary as it was to lay my soul bare to a priest whom I barely knew, I do remember the elation that I felt after having confessed every sin that I could recall up to that point in my life. I felt a tremendous sense of peace with God and a sincere sense that, having been cleansed of all previous sins, I desired to never sin again. Sadly, that sense of jubilation was short-lived. Within hours of that experience I found myself embroiled in a huge fight with my younger sisters and quickly returned to my prior state of being slimed by sin. In retrospect, that experience illustrated to me that the act of confession alone is not sufficient to deliver us from the powerful hold that sin has over our lives. It is only a living, vibrant relationship with the Lord Jesus Christ that can break those chains of bondage. For me, that relationship began on November 2nd, 1985—the day that I surrendered my heart to the Lord Jesus Christ and was supernaturally transferred from the kingdom of this world into the Kingdom of God. Each time I read the thirty-sixth chapter of Ezekiel, I am taken back to that eternal milestone in my life.

Ezekiel was a prophet who prophesied to the nation of Israel in Babylon after they had been taken into captivity by Nebuchadnezzar—a punishment inflicted by God after generations of idolatry, backsliding, and rebellion on the part of the Israelites. As painful as this judgment was, Ezekiel was a prophet of promise who declared that God would not cast away His people forever, but that He still had an amazing plan and future in store for His children. The Israelites had failed time and time and time again to keep the external law of God which had been delivered to them by Moses. Now that they had come to the end of themselves and their human ability to remain faithful to God by their own efforts, the Lord was now promising through the prophetic words of Ezekiel that He was going to establish a brand new covenant in which He alone would do all the work. The Lord alone was going to transform the hearts of those who would come to Him by faith. In the past, He had given the Israelites the external written Law to obey; but under the New Covenant, He was going to write the law internally upon their hearts. Through His Holy Spirit which He would put in them, He was going to transform them into people who would be changed from the inside out instead of from the outside in. When we surrender our lives to Christ, He sends His Holy Spirit to not only lead and guide us externally, but to make His home in our hearts and to transform us into the powerful, sin-overcoming people that He originally created us to be prior to the fall of humanity. Ezekiel foretells this promise in Ezekiel 36:26, when the Word of the Lord promises, "A new heart also will I give you, and a new spirit will I put within you: and I will take away the stony heart out of your flesh, and I will give you an heart of flesh."

On the eve of the ratification of the New Covenant, Jesus promised to His disciples and by extension to us His body, "Now ye are clean through the word which I have spoken unto you" (John 15:3). *Do you feel clean? Do you feel shiny? Do you feel pure? All of these things have been promised to those who will put their trust in Him. If you are not experiencing these sensations, lift up your hands to Him today! Thank Him for His goodness and let Him shower you with His amazing love!*

PRAYER

Lord Jesus, I thank You that I have truly been made clean before You because of what You did for me at the cross. Let me now experience that wonderful cleansing that comes from the knowledge that all of my sins have truly been washed away. Help me to see myself, no longer as a person full of sin and depravity, but as You see me-a pure, holy, blood-washed child of the King! I love You dearly and I worship You with all of my heart.

I pray this in name of Jesus!

DECLARATION

I declare that I am a born-again, child of the Living God. The Lord Jesus Christ, through His death and resurrection, has cleansed me of all sin and all unrighteousness. He has purified me to boldly stand in the presence of Almighty God because I have not only been forgiven, but I have been clothed in His robe of righteousness. I choose to see myself in that righteousness.

I declare this by faith in Jesus' name!

QUESTIONS

1. What are some past sins in your life for which the enemy has continued to try to bring condemnation? Have you given these sins to Jesus by faith?
2. In light of the devotion today, what does it mean to you to be cleansed? In what ways has your understanding of cleansing been expanded?
3. Using an illustration from daily life, how would you explain the fullness of spiritual cleansing?

DAY 38

חֳלִי

choliy

Amazing Suffering, Amazing Healing, Amazing Love!

Surely he hath borne our griefs, and carried our sorrows: yet
we did esteem him stricken, smitten of God, and afflicted.
— Isaiah 53:4

It has been said from the pulpit many times that healings are a great advertisement for the gospel. While I understand the sincere spirit of such a statement, it sadly reflects a common, fundamental understatement of what the Kingdom of God fully entails. Healing is not simply an advertisement for the gospel-healing *is* the gospel! Through the cross, the Lord Jesus Christ made just as much of a provision for all forms of healing as He did for the forgiveness of sins.

In 2 Timothy 3:5, the Apostle Paul declares that in the last times, people will have a form of godliness but deny the power thereof. Unfortunately, many of us in the body of Christ have been duped when it comes to the biblical healing promises. We have been fed a lie, being deceived into settling for the status quo of a watered-down gospel, which, while getting us to heaven, leaves us devoid of the power of God in this life. Even the prophet Isaiah, who prophesied hundreds of years before the first coming of Christ, seemed to have a greater revelation of the then-coming gospel than many New Testament believers have today. Today, we will revisit one of the greatest passages of the Old Testament—the prophecy of the suffering

Servant found in Isaiah 53 and the purpose of His death that He would suffer on the cross of Calvary.

Many of us know that Isaiah 53:5 speaks of how the Lord Jesus Christ was to take upon Himself the sins of the world. He took the punishment sin in our place so that we would stand forgiven before God the Father and have the privilege of spending eternity in heaven. This is infinitely important, but the gospel of salvation—that is, the gospel of forgiveness of sins which focuses primarily or even exclusively on a future life—overlooks the promises of healing and deliverance that the Lord wants us to experience in *this* life. These promises are explicitly given in the preceding verse, Isaiah 53:4. When we understand what Isaiah 53:4 in its marvelous fullness, we can no longer relegate the healing described in Isaiah 53:5 to "spiritual" healing alone.

Surely he hath borne our griefs. The Hebrew word for "griefs" is *choliy*.[204] This word is archaically translated in the King James Version as "griefs," but in modern English it is better rendered "sickness." The root verb is *chalah*, meaning "to be weak or sick."[205] In almost every instance in the Hebrew Bible, *chalah* and *choliy* pertain to physical weaknesses, wounds or sicknesses.

And carried our sorrows. While *choliy* primarily describes physical ailments, the Hebrew word *makowb*, translated "sorrows" in the King James Version, expands the meaning of pain to encompass mental pain and anguish as well.[206] *Makowb* is the noun form of the verb *ka'ab*, meaning, "to be in pain."[207] This word is often used in the Hebrew text to describe a severe pain. The word is never used in a generic sense to describe a state of pain in general, but is always the result of a specific, traumatic event.[208] One scholar writes that this verb "almost always denotes pain or suffering that afflicts the very heart of life, bringing the sufferer close to his final end and damaging or destroying his ties with the circle of the living."[209] Many of us can recall scenes from movies when people fainted when confronted with fearful situations or upon hearing devastating news. In my own life, there are a handful of times that I have been so overwhelmed with fear over specific events that I found myself in a fog. All of these are the types of our sorrows that the Lord Jesus Christ carried for us as He died on the cross.

What is even more striking is the verb that is used which is translated here as "carried." The verb is *çabal*. This is a rare verb in the Hebrew text, meaning "to bear a heavy load."[210] A noun form is "burden-bearer" and is used of heavy laborers who haul large rocks.[211] In Nehemiah 4:4 the word is used in reference to those who were clearing the rubble in the ruined city of Jerusalem to make way for the new wall being built. In 2 Chronicles 2:1 and 2 Chronicles 2:17, the burden-bearers were the workers who cut large blocks out of the quarry, which were to be used in the construction of Solomon's Temple.

Jesus bore all of our sorrows. He did not simply declare them to be gone by the word of His mouth, though He could have easily chosen to do so. He chose instead to bear the full brunt of all the ravages of sin throughout the entire course of human history, down to the very depths of His frail human body—all at the same time. Imagine the agony of passing multiple kidney stones, while having a migraine headache, while having painful boils erupt all over your body, while having your appendix burst, while having ear infections in both ears, while having a complete nervous breakdown, while suffering severe manic depression, while experiencing total rejection, while being tormented under the weight of guilt, while the list goes on and on…If you can even imagine being in such a variegated state of inconceivable agony, you might begin to fathom what the Lord Jesus Christ was experiencing as He was dying on the cross on our behalf. The closest comparable example in Scripture is the account of Job, who lost his entire family, his possessions, his reputation, and his health in the space of a couple days. Yet Job, in all his unimaginable suffering, could not rival what the Lord Jesus Christ endured on the cross in our place.

Are you suffering sickness today? Is your mind or are your emotions in torment? There is absolutely no reason that you should be enduring these things. The Lord Jesus Christ suffered it all, He bore it all, and He triumphed over it all so that we might walk in total freedom! How it grieves Him greatly to see us go through life in pain and misery, when He has already paid the price for these things in full. Give those things to Him, and begin today to walk in the fullness of His promises for your life!

PRAYER

Lord Jesus, I am eternally grateful to You that You died for my sins and that You rose for the dead; but I thank You just as much for taking all of my sicknesses, my weaknesses, and every form of mental and emotional torment that I will ever experience, and You gladly bore them in Your own body on the cross. I thank You that they no longer have a place in my body, in my mind, or in my heart!

I pray this in name of Jesus!

DECLARATION

I declare that I am not only forgiven—I am totally healed! The Lord Jesus Christ took all of my sicknesses, my pains, my weaknesses, my torments, my diseases, my heartaches, my mental brokenness, and He bore them all on the cross of Calvary. The Word of God says in Matthew 8:17, "That it might be fulfilled which was spoken by Esaias the prophet, saying, Himself took our infirmities, and bare our sicknesses." I declare that these things are illegal trespassers in my body, in my mind, and in my being. I will not tolerate what He has already paid! I choose to walk in the freedom of absolute healing!

I declare this by faith in Jesus' name!

QUESTIONS

1. In light of the devotional today, what maladies are you needlessly suffering?
2. How has the message today changed your understanding of the significance of the cross?
3. What miracles are you going to believe for-for yourself or your loved ones?

DAY 39

הלך

halak

The Ultimate Disappearing Act

> And Enoch walked with God:
> and he was not; for God took him.
> – Genesis 5:24

Is there any greater feeling than walking hand-in-hand with the one you love? The intimacy that the Lord Jesus Christ, the lover of our souls, wants us to experience with Him is no less exhilarating than that which we experience with the love of our life. Today we will focus on the obscure account of a man named Enoch who delighted in such a relationship with God—even when the world around him was crumbling in sin, rebellion, and increasing depravity. One writer notes the parallelism that Enoch, the seventh generation in the line of Seth, attained the highest level of holiness, while Lamech, the seventh generation in the line of Cain, attained the lowest level of depravity,[212] boasting of his ability to murder with impunity-even more so than the murdering patriarch from which he was descended (Genesis 4:23-24).

Enoch's story is found early in the genealogy of Adam, as summarized in the fifth chapter of Genesis. Beginning with Adam, Genesis 5 lists several successive generations of people, of whom all we know about their lives is that they lived, had children and died. How sad it is that billions of people likewise live out their lives on earth, having left no more of a legacy than a date of birth and a date of death on their tombstone. Perhaps many of these people accomplished their greatest human ambitions, but after their passing their endeavors fade from remembrance and their gravesites become overgrown with weeds. What is sadly ironic about Genesis 5 is that every person mentioned lived for several hundred years, yet the only memory passed down about their lives is the number of years they lived, and who some of their children were. Among all the people mentioned in Genesis 5, however, two people are singled out for special mention – Enoch and Noah. Here, we will look specifically at the life of Enoch.

After a series of "He lived, he begat and he died" biographies, the writer of Genesis makes special note of Enoch that "He *walked* with God." Although the Scripture tells of how the Lord walked daily in the Garden of Eden in the cool of the day (Genesis 3:8), this is the first mention of anyone in the Bible who lived a life of actively seeking communion with God. This is in spite of the fact that scholars believe that God was still visibly walking and talking audibly with mankind at this point in human history.[213] Sadly, it seems that in the grand scale of humanity, few people in the Old Covenant dispensation demonstrated any desire to know God. There are only two other references to people in the Old Testament who walked with God – Noah (Genesis 6:9) and an ideal priest who is described in Malachi 2:6.[214] The Hebrew verb is *halak,* a very common word which in its broadest sense normally means to "go, come, walk."[215] In this context, however, the verb implies a sense of intimacy or fellowship.[216]

While all the preceding biographies in Genesis 5 end with "and he died," Enoch's biography uniquely ends with the account, "and he was not, for God took him." Ironically, Enoch's lifespan of 365 years was relatively short compared to others of his time. When we look at the lifespan of some of Enoch's contemporaries, we see that Adam lived 930 years (Genesis 5:3); Methuselah, who had the longest lifespan on record, lived 969 years (Genesis 5:27); and Noah lived 950 years (Genesis 9:29). Lest anyone should think that Enoch's "short" lifespan was due to punishment, the biblical author makes it a point to mention twice that Enoch walked with God (Genesis 5:22, 24).[217] Enoch walked so intimately with God that God decided one day to simply translate him directly into His presence. He vanished from this earth and entered into His heavenly home, never tasting death! What a glorious way to go! God is no respecter of persons. If He did this for Enoch, who is to say He will not do it for you and I as well?

In the Hebrew mind, life is often seen as a journey;[218] hence, the verbs "living" and "walking" may be used interchangeably. Metaphorically, "walking" implies a sense of purpose. *Where* one walks may become secondary to the purposeful nature of *how* one walks.[219] Under the surface of the account of Enoch, the writer is implying that Enoch walked purposefully with a specific goal in mind-that goal not being a physical, geographical destination, but the goal of knowing God intimately and ending the journey in His presence.

In many Christian circles, it is assumed that "walking with God" primarily entails a lifestyle of obeying a list of religious rules. One commentary points out that such a lifestyle is actually described in the Old Testament as "walking *before* God" (Genesis 17:1; Genesis 24:40) or "walking *after* God" (Deuteronomy 13:4).[220] The true essence of walking *with* God is relationship with Him, depending upon Him alone as the very sustenance of our being.

When I think about my own experience of walking with God, I think about all the valleys through which I have passed in my life when I had no one to whom to turn but Him, when it was just He and I. I think about my childhood and adolescent years when I was extremely lonely and had virtually no friends. I think about the time when my vehicle broke down in the middle of Texas on Christmas Eve night during a road trip back from Mexico. I think about the four-month wilderness experience that I spent in Dallas after I graduated from seminary, when I found myself in a strange town, unable to find a job and living week-to-week in a transient motel room. I think about the many trials and tribulations and victories through which He has brought me during my many years as a believer. In all these times, I can look back and understand now, though I could not always see at the time, that God always has been, always is, and always will be with me; and when I come to the end of my own "journey," I will see the Lord Jesus face-to-face. Knowing the intimate details of each of those circumstances, He will then reveal to me what He was doing.

Too often, we have little or no concept that God uniquely loves us as individuals. We sometimes tend to see ourselves more as a nameless speck in a mass of humanity than as a person who has been lovingly crafted by our Creator as a trophy in His image. A major part of the problem is that many churches in the Christian world in general do not have this understanding of God's longing to fellowship with us; hence they cannot teach what they do not know. If you feel alienated from God, He is not far away. He longs to make His presence known to us! His presence and love is manifested as we step outside of the routine of daily living and purposefully seek His face in worship and adoration. *Do you feel spiritually dry? Why not take some time to stop what you are doing, turn off the TV, radio, phone or whatever distractions normally clamor for your attention, and set yourself to seeking Him? Tell Him how much you love Him! Tell Him how beautiful He is! Thank Him for His goodness in your life, and wait expectantly for Him to envelope and take you up in His presence! Do not make this a one-time experience, but set your heart to seek His presence everyday and watch how He will transform your heart and your life! Who knows? Perhaps you, too, may be supernaturally ushered directly into His presence forever, just like Enoch!*

PRAYER

*Lord Jesus, I want to know You! I do not simply want to know **about** You. I want to walk with You daily. I want to soak in Your precious, holy presence! I invite you to invade my life with Your glory. Please reveal Yourself to me supernaturally and intimately. Let my walk with You be even deeper than that of Enoch. You have mapped an amazing course and a glorious destiny before me. Thank You for continuing to lead and guide me in Your paths of righteousness.*

I pray this in name of Jesus!

DECLARATION

I declare that I am a unique child of the Living God. He has a unique plan for me like no other. I choose to walk with Him daily. I choose to pursue His presence every single day. I declare that I will triumphantly finish the journey that He has mapped out before me. I will not settle for a life of the ordinary, but I declare that I live life supernaturally in and through Him.

I declare this by faith in Jesus' name!

QUESTIONS

1. How has the devotional today changed your understanding of what it means to walk with Him?
2. Describe a time that you entered deeply into His presence.
3. What has the Lord revealed to you today about His unique love for you?

DAY 40

סוֹד

çowd

He Reveals His Secret to Those Who Love Him

> The secret of the Lord is with them that fear him;
> and he will shew them his covenant.
> – Psalm 25:14

*M*any of us have experienced a level of intimate communication with that one special person, perhaps the love of our life, who is not content with talking with us from a distance but prefers to draw close and speak to us face-to-face or to whisper sweet-nothings into our ear. So it is with God our lover. We are mistakenly taught or conditioned to believe that He only relates to us in a directive or corrective manner and as a result we have no idea how much He longs to know us on the deepest of levels. He wants to share His secrets with us! Today's devotional goes hand-in-hand with the previous devotional from yesterday, which explored what it means to walk with God.

The Hebrew text uses a variety of words throughout the Old Testament which are synonymous with "secret." In this verse, the word is *çowd* (pronounced "sode"), meaning "council" or "counsel."[221] This word is used almost exclusively in the poetic or prophetic books of the Bible—never in narrative accounts; hence, it implicitly carries a poetic nuance.[222] This secrecy is not simply information that is transmitted for utilitarian purposes on a "need-to-know" basis, but is a secrecy that is shared within an intimate relationship between lovers, friends or confidantes. The Hebrew noun *çowd* is rooted in the verb *yaçad*, which, other meanings, means "to lean against, recline, or fix as a pillow against one."[223] The Keil-Delitzsch commentary expands the meaning of *yaçad* to mean "to be or to make tight, firm, compressed," or to express the act of "being closely pressed together for the purpose of secret communication and converse, confidential communion or being together."[224] An obvious biblical image that comes to mind is found in the Gospel of John, when the Apostle John pressed against Jesus' bosom during the Last Supper (John 13:23, 25); In a more intimate context, it is a given that when we are in love, we love to press in close to our lover, in both discourse and intercourse.

The secret here is not to be seen as a single-layered mystery to be understood as a one-time event, but is comprised as a multi-layered truth which is gradually revealed as with the proverbial peeling away of the layers of an onion. The remaining days of our life are woefully inadequate to even begin to scratch the surface of the truth which the Lord desires to fully reveal to us. Charles Spurgeon wrote, "Carnal minds cannot guess what is intended it, and even believers cannot explain it in full words, for it must be felt to be known."[225] Spurgeon continued to explain that "Saints have the key of heaven's hieroglyphics: they can un-riddle celestial enigmas. They are initiated into the fellowship of the skies: they have heard words which it is not possible for them to repeat to their fellows."[226]

The sweet intimacy which God promises is available to all who will draw close to Him by faith. The only qualification is that one fears the Lord. There are some who believe that God cannot be known. Others may believe that He can be known, but only by initiation through a rigorous lifestyle of disciplined prayer, fasting, asceticism, extreme separation from the world, or whatever the defined standard of holiness may be. The reality and the wonderful news is that God earnestly desires to know and to be known by all the people of the earth. For that purpose, He came down to our level in and through the person of His Son Jesus Christ, who for a time laid aside the fullness of His divine glory to live as a man, who submitted Himself to the excruciating death on a cross and who continues to this day to knock on the door of our hearts to invite is into a wonderful relationship of everlasting, intimate communion with Him.

Many years ago, I had the amazing privilege of spending six months in Egypt. I remember one occasion in which I was shopping for souvenirs with a friend of mine who was looking for a specific type of a leather camel bag. We entered into one shop, where the shopkeeper led us under some hanging rugs into a hidden room in the back where he kept his most treasured merchandise which was not visible to the general public. The Gospel writer Matthew writes that when the Lord Jesus Christ died on the cross, "The veil of the temple was rent in twain from the top to the bottom" (Matthew 27:51). This veil refers to the thick curtain which had separated the Most Holy Place in the temple from the rest of the temple. This area had only previously been accessible to the high priest, upon pain of death to any other person who attempted to enter. Jesus, through what He did, has freely granted us access to the most secret place of His presence and glory. He invites us to enter in and experience that glory whenever we desire!

What is the secret to which the psalmist refers? According to the same verse, the secret refers to the covenant. When we see the word "covenant" in the Old Testament, we tend to assume that it refers exclusively to the written Law. Often, this is indeed the correct interpretation, but in this context, the covenant refers to the marriage covenant which the Lord has initiated and entered into with His people. Before the first coming of Christ, this covenant was established between the Lord and the nation of Israel; but after the death and resurrection of Christ, the covenant referred to the marital relationship into which all believers, Jewish and Gentile alike, enter into by faith in His finished work through the cross.

The Apostle Paul marveled that, just as a man and woman become one flesh through marriage, we the Church likewise become one flesh with the Lord Jesus Christ when we receive Him (Ephesians 5:29-32). The depth of the truth of this is beyond the bandwidth of the human mind—it can only be understood by the revelation of the Holy Spirit. The psalmist promises that the Lord will "shew" (or "show" in modern English) His covenant to those who fear Him. The root verb is *yada*, a verb we have previously explored. Here, the verb is used causatively; in other words, the literal text expresses the notion that the Lord will cause the one who fears Him to intimately know or understand His marital covenant which He has initiated. *Yada* is an intimate verb often used in the Old Testament as a euphemism with reference to sexual intercourse. He will not only make us to see the covenant in a theoretical or a flat theological sense, but He will make us to thoroughly understand it on the deepest of levels.

Are you in on the secret? Do you truly know what it means to be in the covenant of holy matrimony with the Lord Jesus Christ? He longs to reveal Himself to you! He longs to bring you into the deepest places of intimacy with Him! Simply open your heart to Him in worship, and expect amazing downloads of divine secrets through His Holy Spirit!

PRAYER

Lord Jesus, I want to know Your secrets! I want to know in the deepest core of my being what You have done for me and what are the privileges of son-ship or daughter-ship that I have been freely granted in You! Thank you for not only saving me from hell, but for making me Your royal heir. Thank You for the amazing promises that You have in store for me and thank You for pouring out Your greatest blessings upon me every single day!

I pray this in name of Jesus!

DECLARATION

I declare that I am in marital covenant with the Lord Jesus Christ. I, as part of His Church, am His bride and He is my Bridegroom (Revelation 21:2, 9; Revelation 22:17). Because I am His beloved bride, He reveals the deepest and most intimate of secrets to me. I am my Beloved's and He is mine (Song of Solomon 6:3; Song of Solomon 7:10) and I enjoy perfect marital bliss in His holy presence, every single moment of every single day.

I declare this by faith in Jesus' name!

QUESTIONS

1. What does it mean to you to be the bride of the Lord Jesus Christ?
2. What secrets has He revealed to you?
3. What are some identifiable ways that you have not been walking in the fullness of your privileges as the bride of Christ? What are some scriptural promises that speak of those privileges?

DAY 41

עזר

azar

Our Spouse Is More than a Sidekick

And the Lord God said, It is not good that the man should be alone;
I will make him an help meet for him.
— Genesis 2:18

It has been cynically said, "All men are created equal, but some are more equal than others." One of the most glaring results of the fall of humanity is that, throughout human history, it has produced a pecking order of so-called superiors who dominate over subservient subordinates. Humanity created in the image of God has been marred through every imaginable form of dominance of one over another, be it international or interpersonal. This is certainly true with regard to how males have often treated females as inferior beings. I remember a time that I was staying as a guest at an orphanage in Mexico (a truly *machismo* culture), when one of the young man asked me if I wanted some breakfast. When I responded, "Yes," he abruptly turned to a young girl in the kitchen and, speaking to her as a slave, commanded her to my utter embarrassment, "You! Make him some breakfast!" On another occasion at the same orphanage, I was helping clean up some tables after a party when a teenager wagged her finger at me and chided, "Men don't clean!" Though varying in degrees from culture to culture, the role of the female has often been deemed to be inferior to that of the male. Today we will go back to the beginning of the human narrative to set the record straight as to what the role of the spouse was originally intended to be.

In Genesis, the Scripture tells how God created man in His image and in the very same sentence defines what the role of humanity was to be-to exercise dominion over the earth (Genesis 1:26). The dominion over the earth was not an afterthought—it was the Lord's plan from the very beginning, the very purpose for which humanity was created. It is fascinating that God gave the command to multiply in Genesis 1:28, before the woman was created. This may seem illogical to the natural mind; hence rabbinical teachers have struggled with what form of a man Adam may have been.

In any case, having created Adam, the Lord looked down and saw that it was not good that he was alone. This is not to say that Adam was lonely, because loneliness came into the world only after the fall of humanity, which had not yet occurred at this point in time. Moreover, to say that Adam was lonely would imply that God Himself was not sufficient to meet all of Adam's emotional needs. Such an assertion would be affront to God! The real "problem" was that God had created Adam for the purpose of establishing His kingdom over all the earth-a daunting task for one person alone. Hence, God declared that He would create someone as a help-not simply as an assistant or sidekick, but one who would be worthy to come alongside him as his equal. The Hebrew verb used is *azar*, meaning to "help, succour."[227] It is the sort of assistance that relieves a person from being spread too thin and having to do everything in a hasty, sloppy manner.

The expression "an help meet for him" is a simplified translation of something profound that is being expressed in the Hebrew text. Taken together with the verb *neged*, the Hebrew phrase in its totality describes this person as one who helps like or as who is being opposite to, in front of, or before him.[228] *Neged* also means "to be conspicuous."[229] The idea being conveyed is that the woman was created as an absolute equal to the man, as opposed to being the weaker sex.

Prior to the creation of the woman, the Lord had called all the birds and all the land animals to Adam to see if he would find any worthy to fulfill this role, but none was found. Adam had seriously considered each "candidate." Contrary to the assumption that Adam quickly and randomly named the animals as they were brought to him, the truth is that he thoughtfully studied each and carefully named them on the basis of the most dominant attributes that stood out to him.[230] Even after having evaluated all the birds and the land animals on the face of the earth, Adam had been unable to find among them a suitable equal to assist him in the commission to extend the Kingdom of God over all the earth. When Adam finally saw the woman, he immediately saw a glorious reflection of himself in her; hence, upon seeing her he excitedly exclaimed the very first recorded words uttered by any human: "This is now bone of my bones, and flesh of my flesh: she shall be called Woman, because she was taken out of Man" (Genesis 2:23). The true sense of equality is further emphasized by the fact that she was taken out of Adam's side, not out of his back or out of a lower part of his body. Prior to this moment, the man was only known as *adam*, the Hebrew term referring to man or humanity in general.[231] By virtue of naming his wife *ishshah* (meaning "female"),[232] he now also names himself *iysh* (meaning "male"),[233] prompting one Jewish commentator to observe that Adam discovered his own manhood at the moment when he first faced the woman who was to be his partner.[234] It is significant that, in the Hebrew text, *ishshah* contains a double consonant in the middle of the word. The double consonant is a grammatical way of expressing intensity. Adam was clearly awed and speechless by the woman whom God had given to him!

    I believe that there is a deeper truth being revealed here than that of the marital bonding between a man and a woman. That truth speaks of the greater marital relationship into which we as believers enter with the Lord Jesus Christ when we put our faith in Him. Ephesians 5:29-32 declares, "For no man ever yet hated his own flesh; but nourisheth and cherisheth it, even as the Lord the church: For we are members of his body, of his flesh, and of his bones. For this cause shall a man leave his father and mother, and shall be joined unto his wife, and they two shall be one flesh. This is a great mystery: but I speak concerning Christ and the church." We the Church of the Lord Jesus Christ are His bride (Revelation 21:2, 9; Revelation 22:17). In the same way that the first Adam was excited upon seeing his wife, so the Lord Jesus Christ, the last Adam (1 Corinthians 15:45) is no less enthralled at the radiant, resplendent sight of His glorious bride, the

Church. It is for this very reason that He joyfully went to the cross on our behalf (Hebrews 12:2). Jesus prayed that our unity in the Father and Him would be no less binding than that which exists between the Father and Him (John 17:20-23).

Do you feel like a mere slave of God, a simple tool in His hands to fulfill His purposes? Sadly, many believers do not realize that they are truly seated in heavenly places with Him (Ephesians 2:6). They do not realize that in Him they have been promoted from the status of a servant to that of an intimate friend (John 15:15). Above all, the inheritance of believers is that they are wedded to Him in holy matrimony. *Do you go through times of feeling worthless? Be encouraged in knowing that you are truly one in Him! Be encouraged that He rejoices in you and in everything about you! He passionately loves you! As Adam rejoiced at the sight of the woman, so the Lord Jesus Christ rejoices in you, His chosen, lovely bride!*

PRAYER

Lord Jesus, I pray that You will show me how precious I truly am in Your sight. Please open my spiritual eyes to see myself through Your eyes. Show me the beauty and the splendor that You see in me. Please reveal the truth of what it means to be Your bride and to truly be one with You.

I pray this in name of Jesus!

DECLARATION

I declare that I am the bride of Christ and He is my Groom. I am one in Him and He is one in me. He loves me passionately and calls me His intimate friend. He rejoices over me with singing. I am filled with a love and an enthralling passion that compels me to share His love and glory with others—both those who know Him and those who do not. I choose to participate in the Great Commission to extend His Kingdom over all the earth—no longer out of a sense of duty but as an overflowing response to His amazing love.

I declare this by faith in Jesus' name!

QUESTIONS

1. In what ways have you seen yourself as less than how Christ sees you?
2. How has the devotional today transformed the way that you see your spouse?
3. How has the devotional today transformed your understanding of your relationship with the Lord Jesus Christ?

DAY 42

בבה

babah

We Are the Apple of His Eye

For thus saith the Lord of hosts; After the glory hath he sent me unto the nations which spoiled you: for he that toucheth you toucheth the apple of his eye.
– Zechariah 2:8

There is perhaps no part of our body of which we are more protective than our eyes. We may endanger our ears by listening to loud music; we may wear down our back through heavy lifting; we may eat foods laden with fat that endanger our heart; and we may knowingly do many other things that endanger our health or bodies, but we are diligent to take special care of our eyes. We simply cannot bear the thought of losing vision in one or both of our eyes. Think about it…when we hear a sudden loud noise, when we see an object coming in our direction or even when we sneeze, we instinctively close our eyes. Along the same lines, in several instances of the Old Testament, the Lord calls us "the apple of His eye" to vividly demonstrate the special care that He takes over us and in so doing reveals the jealous love that He has for us. Over one hundred years ago, the great preacher Charles Spurgeon, in his voluminous commentary *The Treasury of David*, quoted Socrates in highlighting the wonder of how the Creator built several layers of protection into the face for the sole purpose of guarding the most vulnerable eyes.[235] The classical Greek writer Xenophon, almost under inspiration, marvel's at God's amazing handiwork:

"And besides all this, do you not think this looks like a matter of foresight, this closing of the delicate orbs of sight with eyelids as with folding doors, which, when there is need to use them for any purpose, can be thrown wide open and firmly closed again in sleep? and, that even the winds of heaven may not visit them too roughly, this planting of the eyelashes as a protecting screen? (6) this coping of the region above the eyes with cornice-work of eyebrow so that no drop of sweat fall from the head and injure them?"[236]

In several passages in the Bible, the Lord lovingly refers to His people as the "apple of His eye." The exact biblical meaning of this expression has been debated because it is not clearly defined. Perhaps the reason for the ambiguity is that different Hebrew words are used to express the same sentiment, depending on the passage. In today's devotional, we will look at several different passages whose unique word choice is rich in imagery.

We begin in today's primary scriptural reference found in Zechariah 2:8. The Book of Zechariah was written by the prophet Zechariah, who was a descendent of the Old Covenant priesthood. By the time his prophecy was recorded, the Israelites had been in captivity for several years and were growing increasingly discouraged that they no longer had a future as a nation. In response to their anguish, the Lord revealed a series of visions to Zechariah to communicate to them that, although they were in exile because of the sins of previous generations, He was not through with them. Rather, there was coming a day when He was going to judge the very nations that had plundered them, destroyed their land, and carried them off. In speaking this promise, the Lord declared that those who touch His people touch the very apple of His eye. Although this English expression is found elsewhere in the Old Testament, the Hebrew *babah*, translated "apple," is found only here.[237] The literal meaning is "opening" or "hollow," rooted in the Hebrew verb *nabab*, meaning "to hollow out."[238] Buried within the simple anatomical reference, however, is a play on words, a precious term of endearment being spoken to His people. *Babah* also means "baby," an onomatopoeia which imitates the sound of baby talk; therefore, the Hebrew phrase can also mean "the child or baby of His eye."[239] People love babies! Most would not dream of carelessly tossing a baby around and no self-respecting parent would dream of leaving an infant to fend for himself or herself—how much less would the Lord neglect His own darling, precious babies! By extension, we, too, who are believers in the Lord Jesus Christ partake of the promises of Abraham (John 1:12; Galatians 3:9, 13). That being the case, we, too, have become the apple of His eye.

Another biblical reference to the apple of His eye is found in Deuteronomy 32:10 when the Lord relates how He tenderly cared for His children the Israelites during their vulnerable wilderness wanderings through the harsh, howling wasteland. Here, instead of *babah*, the writer Moses, under the inspiration of the Holy Spirit, chooses the Hebrew word *iyshown*. Again, this Hebrew expression is found in no other place in the Bible. In this case, "*-own*" is added to the root word *iysh*, meaning man (in the sense of a male) to change it to a term of endearment. In so doing He looks affectionately upon His people as the "little man" of His eye. Several years ago, I knew a young lady who always loved to call her beloved toddler son her "little man." I believe that the Lord is likewise expressing the same sentiment toward His beloved child, the nation of Israel.

Still another reference to our being the apple of His eye is highlighted in Psalm 17:8. In the midst of persecution at the hands of his enemies, King David prays for deliverance and asks that the Lord keep him as the apple of His eye. In this case, the Hebrew word which has been rendered "apple" in English is *bath*, which actually means "daughter,"[240] so he is actually saying, "Keep me as the daughter of Your eye." It is fascinating that King David, the idealized picture of manhood in the Bible, would compare himself in any way to being a daughter of God, but this illustrates the intimacy that he enjoyed in the presence of the Lord whom he so passionately loved.

Any way you look at it, every biblical reference to our being the apple of His eye reveals the amazing, intimate, jealous love which the Lord personally feels toward each and every one of us, His children. Sadly, many have not embraced the fullness of their true identity, and see themselves as nothing more than rotten apples. When I was young,

I remember that our next door neighbors at that time had an old crabapple tree in their front yard. We were not allowed to eat the apples because they were not good for us, though we often ate them anyway. Although they were inedible, one redeeming use for them was that we would sometimes have apple wars and throw them at some mean neighborhood kids whom we did not like. Sadly, we as believers are prone to see ourselves as having little more value than to be thrown away. Beloved, nothing could be further from the truth! God created us in His image so that we might know Him and enjoy wonderful fellowship with Him.

It has often been said that the apple does not fall far from the tree. Unfortunately, this expression often means that we tend to inherit the faults of our parents; but in the context of Zechariah 2:8, the same expression can and should be taken to mean that as He our Heavenly Father is, so are we His children. We are His holy offspring. We come from Him and therefore we are extensions of His glory on the earth. How about you? How do you see yourself—as the precious apple of His eye, or a squishy, worm-infested apple rotting in the grass and crawling with bugs? Know for certain Jesus truly loves you and desires that you rise up in your identity as a beautiful, royal child of the King. According to Ephesians 2:6, we, His beloved believers, have been seated in heavenly places with Him. *You are the apple of His eye! Embrace that truth and walk worthy of the calling to which He has called you!*

PRAYER

Lord Jesus, I pray that You will open my eyes, that I might see myself as You truly see me-as the apple of Your eye. Please reveal to me the truth of what that means and empower me every moment of every day to live up to and walk in that identity. I pray that You will supernaturally reveal the depths of Your amazing love for me. Let me experience divine encounters with You!

I pray this in name of Jesus!

DECLARATION

I declare that I am beloved of God. He loves me passionately and I am truly the apple of His eye. I am a sweet, golden, delicious apple to be enjoyed by Him-not a rotten, bitter crabapple to be mulched or thrown. He protects me as He does His own eyes; He cherishes me like He does His own son or daughter; and He proudly sees me as His little man. I choose by faith to embrace my identity in Him, moment by moment and day by day.

I declare this by faith in Jesus' name!

QUESTIONS

1. Have you ever asked the Lord how He truly sees you? What did He show you about yourself?
2. Which description of the apple of His eye ministers to you the most and why?
3. What other scripture verses come to mind when you meditate on today's devotional?

GLOSSARY OF HEBREW WORDS USED IN PRICELESS STONES

ENGLISH-HEBREW GLOSSARY

A

abandon (*azab*)
abominable (*shiqqutz*)
Almighty (*Shadday*)
almond (*shaqed*)
apple (*babah*)
apple (*iyshown*)

B

barb (*tsen, tsinnah*)
be, become (*havah*)
be, become (*hayah*)
be clean (*taher*)
be conspicuous (*neged*)
be fat (*dashen*)
be heavy (*kabed*)
be high, conspicuous (*naças*)
be in front of (*neged*)
be in pain (*ka'ab*)
be jealous (*qana*)
be just, righteous (*tsadaq*)
be mighty (*gabar*)
be opposite to (*neged*)
be pure (*taher*)
be red (*adom*)
be red (*adem*)
be sick, weak (*chalah*)
be silent (*charash*)
be strong (*gabar*)
be surpassing (*pala*)
be white (*laban*)
bear a heavy load (*çabal*)
blood (*dam*)
breast (*shad*)
breast (*shod*)
burden-bearer (*çabal*)

C

cleave (*dabaq*)
come (*halak*)
covenant (*b^{e}riyth*)
creeping thing (*remes*)
crown (*atarah*)

D

daughter (*bath*)
destroy (*shadad*)
dine (*barah*)
dust (*aphar*)

E

eat (*barah*)

F

fail *(raphah)*
fatness (*dashen*)
fear (*yare*)
female (*ishshah*)
food (*biryah*)
form (*yatsar*)
forsake (*azab*)

G

glue (*debeq*)
go (*halak*)
God (*El*)
gold (*zahab*)
goodness (*cheçed*)
growl (*hagah*)

H

have success (*sakal*)
heal (*raphah*)
hear (*sh^{e}ma*)
help (*azar*)
hollow (*babah*)
hollow out (*nabab*)
holy (*kadesh, qadesh*)
hook (*tsinnah*)
hope (*tiqvah*)

I

J

jealous (*qanna*)
joy (*simchah*)

K

know (*yada*)

L

lamp (*ner*)
lean against (*yaçad*)

leave (*azab*)
light (*owr*)
little man (*iyshown*)
The Lord (*Adonai*)
The Lord (*Jehovah, Y^{e}hovah*)
The Lord has saved (*Y^{e}howshua*)
The Lord is my banner (*Jehovah-Nissi, Y^{e}hovah-Nicciy*)
The Lord is peace (*Jehovah-Shalom, Y^{e}hovah-Shalowm*)
The Lord is there (*Jehovah-Shammah, Y^{e}hovah-Shammah*)
The Lord of Hosts (*Jehovah-Tsabbaoth, Y^{e}hovah-Tsabbaoth*)
The Lord Our Righteousness (*Jehovah-Tsidkenu, Y^{e}hovah-Tsidqenuw*)
The Lord who heals (*Jehovah-Raphah, Yahveh-Raphah*)
The Lord will provide (*Jehovah-Jireh, Y^{e}hovah-Yireh*)

M

male (*iysh*)
man, mankind (*adam*)
meditate (*hagah*)
menstrual (*iddah*)
might (*m^{e}od*)
mighty (*gibbor*)

moan (*hagah*)
Most High (*Elyon*)
muse (*hagah*)

N

The Name (*Hashem*)

O

olive, olive tree (*zayith*)
opening (*babah*)

P

pain (*makowb*)
peace (*shalom*)
praise (*halal*)
Praise the Lord (*Hallelujah*)
prevail (*gabar*)
prosper (*tsalach*)
pure (*tahor*)
purify (*barar*)

Q

R

recline (*yaçad*)
rejoice (*giyl*)
rejoice (*samach*)
rejoice (*siys*)
relax (*raphah*)
Righteousness of the Lord
(*Tsedekiah, Zedekiah*)
ringing cry (*rinnah*)

S

save (*yasha*)
secret (*çowd*)
see (*ra'ah*)
select (*barar*)
set apart (*badal*)
shadow (*tsel*)
shield (*tsinnah*)
shine (*halal*)
sickness (*choliy*)
sink (*raphah*)
sorrow (*makowb*)
soul (*nephesh*)
speak (*hagah*)
split (*palag*)
sprinkle (*nazah*)
sprinkle (*zaraq*)
standard (*nes*)
stork (*chaçiydah*)
surround (*atar*)

T

there (*sham*)
think (*chashab*)
thorn (*tsen*)
thought (*machshaba*)
thunder (*ra'am*)
treasure (*s^{e}gullah*)

U

us (*anu*)
utter (*hagah*)

V

voice (*qol*)

W

wage war (*tsabah*)
wait for (*qavah*)
wake (*shaqad*)
walk (*halak*)

with (*im*)
With us is God (*Immanuel*)
wonderful (*peliy*)

X

Y

Z

HEBREW-ENGLISH GLOSSARY

A

adam (*man, mankind*)
adem (*be red*)
adom (*be red*)
Adonai (*The Lord*)
Adonai-Nicciy (*The Lord is my banner*)
Adonai-Raphah (*The Lord who heals*)
Adonai-Shalowm (*The Lord is peace*)
Adonai-Shammah (*The Lord is there*)
Adonai-Tsabbaoth (*The Lord of Hosts*)
Adonai-Tsidqenuw (*The Lord Our Righteousness*)
Adonai-Yireh (*The Lord will provide*)
anu (*us*)
aphar (*dust*)
atar (*surround*)
atarah (*crown*)
azab (*leave, abandon, forsake*)
azar (*help, succour*)

B

babah (*apple, opening, hollow*)
badal (*set apart*)
barah (*eat, dine*)
barar (*purify, select*)
bath (*daughter*)
bᵉriyth (*covenant*)
biryah (*food*)

C

çabal (*bear a heavy load, burden-bearer*)
chaçiydah (*stork*)
chalah (*be sick, weak*)
charash (*be silent*)
chashab (*think*)
cheçed (*mercy*)
choliy (*sickness*)
çowd (*secret*)

D

dabaq (*cleave*)
dam (*blood*)
dashen (*be fat, grow fat, fatness*)
debeq (*glue*)

E

El (*God*)
Elyon (*Most High*)

F

G

gabar (to be strong, mighty; to prevail)
gibbor (*mighty*)
giyl (*rejoice*)

H

hagah (*meditate, moan, growl, utter, speak, muse*)
halak (*go, come, walk*)
halal (*praise, shine*)
Hallelujah (*Praise the Lord*)
hashab (*think*)
Hashem (*The Name*)
havah (*to be, become*)
hayah (*to be, become*)

I

iddah (*menstrual*)
im (*with*)
Immanuel (*With us is God*)
ishshah (*female*)
iysh (*male*)
iyshown (*apple, little man*)

J

Jehovah (*The Lord*)
Jehovah-Jireh (*The Lord will provide*)
Jehovah-Nissi (*The Lord is my banner*)
Jehovah-Raphah (*The Lord who heals*)
Jehovah-Shalom (*The Lord is peace*)
Jehovah-Shammah (*The Lord is there*)
Jehovah-Tsabbaoth (*The Lord of Hosts*)
Jehovah-Tsidkenu (*The Lord Our Righteousness*)

K

ka'ab (*be in pain*)
kabed (*be heavy*)
kadesh (*holy*)

L

laban (*be white*)

M

machshaba (*thought*)
makowb (*pain, sorrow*)
m^{e}od (*might*)

N

nabab (*hollow out*)
naças (*be high, conspicuous*)
nazah (*sprinkle*)
nes (*standard*)
neged (*be in front of, opposite to, conspicuous*)
nephesh (*soul*)
ner (*lamp*)

O

owr (*light*)

P

palag (*split*)
pala (*to be surpassing*)
peliy (*wonderful*)

Q

qadesh (*holy*)
qana (*be jealous*)
qanna (*jealous*)
qavah (*wait for*)
qol (*voice*)

R

ra'ah (*see*)
ra'am (*thunder*)
raphah (*heal*)
raphah (*sink, relax, fail*)
remes (*creeping thing*)
rinnah *(ringing cry)*

S

sakal (*have success*)
samach (*rejoice*)
sᵉgullah (*treasure*)
shad (*breast*)
shadad (*destroy*)
Shadday (*Almighty*)
shalom (*peace*)

sham (*there*)
shaqad (*wake*)
shaqed (*almond*)
shᵉma (*hear*)
shiqqutz (*abominable*)
shod (*breast*)
simchah (*joy*)
siys (*rejoice*)

T

taher (*be clean, pure*)
tahor (*pure*)
tiqvah (*hope*)
tsabah (*wage war*)
tsadaq (*be just, righteous*)
tsalach (*prosper*)
Tsedekiah (*Righteousness of the Lord*)
tsel (*shadow*)
tsen (*thorn, barb*)
tsinnah (*shield, hook, barb*)

U

V

W

X

Y

yaçad (*lean against, recline*)
yada (*know*)
yare (*fear*)

yasha (*save*)
yatsar (*form*)
Y^e hovah (*The Lord*)
Y^e hovah-Nicciy (*The Lord is my banner*)
Y^e hovah-Raphah (*The Lord who heals*)
Y^e hovah-Shalowm (*The Lord is peace*)
Y^e hovah-Shammah (*The Lord is there*)
Y^e hovah-Tsabbaoth (*The Lord of Hosts*)
Y^e hovah-Tsidqenuw (*The Lord Our Righteousness*)
Y^e hovah-Yireh (*The Lord will provide*)
Y^e howshua *(The Lord has saved)*

Z

zahab (*gold*)
zaraq (*sprinkle*)
zayith (*olive, olive tree*)
Zedekiah (*Righteousness of the Lord*)

SCRIPTURE INDEX

1 Chronicles 10:7 113
1 Chronicles 29:3 100
1 Corinthians 15:45 134
1 Corinthians 2:1-5 105
1 John 4:4 114
1 John 4:8 70
1 John 5:4-5 86
1 Kings 1:4 22
1 Peter 2:17 54
1 Peter 2:9 .... 37, 97
1 Samuel 1:19 22
1 Samuel 17 88
1 Samuel 17:40 88
1 Samuel 17:44 88
1 Samuel 17:45 88
1 Samuel 17:7 88
1 Samuel 23:26 24
1 Samuel 31:7 113
2 Chronicles 2:1 125
2 Chronicles 2:17 125
2 Chronicles 26 91
2 Chronicles 3:1 76
2 Chronicles 31:21 28
2 Chronicles 36:11-13 91
2 Chronicles 36:17-19 92
2 Corinthians 12:9 89
2 Corinthians 5:18-21 97
2 Corinthians 5:21 ..... 16, 93
2 Corinthians 9:8 78
2 Kings 2:12 33
2 Kings 24:1 108
2 Kings 24:15-17 91
2 Kings 24:17 92
2 Kings 24:8-16 108
2 Kings 24-25 91
2 Kings 25:1-11 108
2 Kings 25:7 92
2 Kings 7:7 113
2 Timothy 3:2 33
2 Timothy 3:5 124
Amos 4:2 25
Colossians 1:18 39
Colossians 1:21-22 77
Colossians 2:15 86
Colossians 2:21 65
Daniel 1:1-7 108
Deuteronomy 13:4 128
Deuteronomy 32:10 137
Deuteronomy 32:39 73
Deuteronomy 6:4-5 ... 12, 21
Deuteronomy 6:4-9 12
Deuteronomy 6:5 13
Deuteronomy 7:6-7 100
Ecclesiastes 2:8 100
Ecclesiastes 4:9-10 110
Ephesians 2:1-10 93
Ephesians 2:6 .... 135, 138
Ephesians 3:20 .. 48, 78, 103
Ephesians 5:25-33 118
Ephesians 5:29-32 .... 44, 131, 134
Ephesians 5:32 118
Exodus 15:26 79
Exodus 17 85
Exodus 17:10-13 85
Exodus 17:15 85

Exodus 19:3 109	Genesis 17:10 96
Exodus 19:5 ...... 97, 99, 100	Genesis 17:7 95
Exodus 20:12 33	Genesis 2:18 133
Exodus 25 121	Genesis 2:23 .... 44, 134
Exodus 26:33 37	Genesis 2:24 44
Exodus 3:13-14 72	Genesis 2:7 .... 41, 42
Exodus 3:14 88	Genesis 22:14 .... 76, 77
Exodus 30:3 121	Genesis 22:2 76
Exodus 31:4 67	Genesis 24:16 22
Exodus 33:19 73	Genesis 24:40 128
Exodus 34:14 118	Genesis 3:8 127
Ezekiel 1:28 72	Genesis 38:26 22
Ezekiel 36:25 121	Genesis 4:1 22
Ezekiel 36:25-26 120	Genesis 4:17 22
Ezekiel 36:26 122	Genesis 4:23-24 127
Ezekiel 36:29 62	Genesis 4:25 22
Ezekiel 37:23 62	Genesis 43:27 64
Ezekiel 48:35 82	Genesis 5 .... 127, 128
Ezekiel 8:10 .... 66, 108, 109	Genesis 5:22, 24 128
Ezekiel 8:12 109	Genesis 5:24 127
Ezekiel 8:2-3 108	Genesis 5:27 128
Galatians 3:13 86	Genesis 5:3 128
Galatians 3:9, 13 137	Genesis 6:9 127
Galatians 5:22-23 36	Genesis 8:11 105
Genesis 1:14-16 51	Genesis 9:29 128
Genesis 1:26 133	Hebrews 10:27 53
Genesis 1:27 56	Hebrews 12:2 .... 45, 134
Genesis 1:28 133	Hebrews 13:5 .... 83, 113
Genesis 1:6 37	Hebrews 13:8 60
Genesis 1:7 30	Hebrews 4:16 .... 54, 77
Genesis 12 96	Hosea 2:19 118
Genesis 15 96	Isaiah 1:18 .... 15, 120
Genesis 15:8 96	Isaiah 11:10 86
Genesis 15:9-17 96	Isaiah 2:22 117
Genesis 17 96	Isaiah 29:16 41
Genesis 17:1 128	Isaiah 40:12 60

Isaiah 40:31	67
Isaiah 41:7	44
Isaiah 43:10, 13	73
Isaiah 44:5-6	73
Isaiah 48:12	73
Isaiah 5:20	28
Isaiah 51:5	67
Isaiah 53	80, 124
Isaiah 53:2	105
Isaiah 53:4	80, 124
Isaiah 53:5	79, 124
Isaiah 54:5	118
Isaiah 55:2	103
Isaiah 55:8-9	112
Isaiah 62:5	118
Isaiah 64:5-6	62
Isaiah 64:6	92
Isaiah 7:14	83
Isaiah 8:8	83
Isaiah 9:6	64
James 2:19	72
Jeremiah 11:16	105
Jeremiah 14:8	67
Jeremiah 17:13	67
Jeremiah 17:5-7	78
Jeremiah 18:4-6	41
Jeremiah 19:5	66
Jeremiah 23:5-6	91, 92
Jeremiah 29:10	66
Jeremiah 29:11	66, 67
Jeremiah 31:31-33	96
Jeremiah 4:14	62
Job 18:6	51
Job 24:14-15	117
Job 29:3	51
Job 37:21	121
Job 5:5	25
Job 7:2	18
John 1:12	137
John 13:19	73
John 13:23, 25	130
John 14:12	113
John 14:27	64
John 14:9	80
John 15:15	135
John 15:16	106
John 15:3	122
John 15:5	13
John 17:20-23	134
John 18:5-8	73
John 18:6	73
John 6:37	16
John 8:24, 28	73
John 8:58	73
John 8:59	73
Jonah 4:6	18
Joshua 1	27
Joshua 1:5	112
Joshua 1:8	27, 28
Judges 13:17	48
Judges 13:18	47
Judges 13:22	47
Judges 19:25	22
Judges 6:24	73
Leviticus 14:51	121
Leviticus 15:19-33	92
Leviticus 20	37
Leviticus 20:23-25	37
Leviticus 20:26	36, 37
Leviticus 3:16-17	103
Luke 2:13	88
Luke 4:18-19	80

Malachi 2:6 127	Psalm 107:12-13 62
Malachi 3:3 121	Psalm 118:6 83
Mark 16:18 80	Psalm 119 50
Mark 4:10 50	Psalm 119:105 .... 50, 51
Matthew 10:30 114	Psalm 136 69
Matthew 11:20 21, 23 60	Psalm 136:1 69
Matthew 13:52 100	Psalm 136:10-22 69
Matthew 13:54, 58 60	Psalm 136:23-24 69
Matthew 14:2 60	Psalm 136:25 70
Matthew 25:1-13 105	Psalm 136:4-9 69
Matthew 27:46 109	Psalm 139:13-18 100
Matthew 27:51 131	Psalm 139:7-10 60
Matthew 8:16 80	Psalm 139:7-8 83
Matthew 8:17 .... 80, 126	Psalm 145:19 62
Numbers 14:10 112	Psalm 148:1-4 88
Numbers 14:6-9 112	Psalm 150 116
Numbers 16:46-49 39	Psalm 150:6 116
Numbers 16-17 39	Psalm 17:8 137
Numbers 17:8 39	Psalm 22 109
Numbers 6:24-26 64	Psalm 22:1 109
Numbers 6:26 64	Psalm 22:22 109
Philippians 2:10-11 72	Psalm 24:7-8 59
Philippians 2:9-10 86	Psalm 24:8 59
Philippians 2:9-11 89	Psalm 25:14 130
Philippians 4:19 76	Psalm 29 .... 30, 31, 64
Proverbs 1:7 53	Psalm 29:3 .... 30, 31
Proverbs 10:22 65	Psalm 34:18 62
Proverbs 11:25 103	Psalm 34:6 62
Proverbs 13:4 103	Psalm 46:1 73
Proverbs 22:5 25	Psalm 5 24
Proverbs 28:13 28	Psalm 5:12 24
Proverbs 28:25 103	Psalm 51:9 16
Proverbs 3:5-6 21	Psalm 71:5 67
Psalm 103:20-21 88	Psalm 91:1 .... 18, 19
Psalm 103:3 79	Revelation 1:17 72
Psalm 104:20 109	Revelation 1:4, 8 73

Revelation 12:10 45
Revelation 16:5 73
Revelation 21:2, 9 .... 118, 132, 134
Revelation 22:17 .... 118, 132, 134
Revelation 4:8 73
Revelation 6:15-17 18
Romans 10:9-10, 13 71

Romans 3:23 15
Romans 8:28 112
Romans 8:31 83
Song of Solomon 6:3 132
Song of Solomon 7:10 .. 132
Zechariah 2:8 .... 136, 138
Zephaniah 3:17 .... 56, 57

BIBLIOGRAPHY

Books

Anderson, David A. *All the Trees and Woody Plants of the Bible.* Word Books, Publisher, 1979.

Arthur, Kay. *The New Inductive Study Bible.* Eugene, OR: Precept Ministries International, Published by Harvest House Publishers, 2000.

The Babylonian Talmud, Seder Mo'ed, Ta'anith. Trans. Rabbi Dr. I Epstein. London: The Soncino Press, 1938.

Block, Daniel I. *The Book of Ezekiel, Chapters 25-48.* Grand Rapids, MI: William B. Eerdmans Publishing Company, 1997.

Botterweck, G. Johannes and Helmer Ringgren. *Theological Dictionary of the Old Testament*, Vol. I, Trans. John T. Willis. Grand Rapids, MI: William B. Eerdmans Publishing Company, 1977.

Botterweck, G. Johannes and Helmer Ringgren. *Theological Dictionary of the Old Testament*, Vol. II, Trans. John T. Willis. Grand Rapids, MI: William B. Eerdmans Publishing Company, 1975.

Botterweck, G. Johannes and Helmer Ringgren. *Theological Dictionary of the Old Testament*, Vol. III, Trans. John T. Willis and Geoffrey W. Bromiley. Grand Rapids, MI: William B. Eerdmans Publishing Company, 1978.

Botterweck, G. Johannes and Helmer Ringgren. *Theological Dictionary of the Old Testament*, Vol. IV, Trans. David E. Green. Grand Rapids, MI: William B. Eerdmans Publishing Company, 1980.

Botterweck, G. Johannes and Helmer Ringgren. *Theological Dictionary of the Old Testament*, Vol. V, Trans. David E.

Green. Grand Rapids, MI: William B. Eerdmans Publishing Company, 1986.

Botterweck, G. Johannes and Helmer Ringgren. *Theological Dictionary of the Old Testament*, Vol. VI, Trans. David E. Green. Grand Rapids, MI: William B. Eerdmans Publishing Company, 1990.

Botterweck, G. Johannes, Helmer Ringgren and Heinz-Josef Fabry. *Theological Dictionary of the Old Testament*, Vol. VII, Trans. David E. Green. Grand Rapids, MI: William B. Eerdmans Publishing Company, 1995.

Botterweck, G. Johannes, Helmer Ringgren and Heinz-Josef Fabry. *Theological Dictionary of the Old Testament*, Vol. IX, Trans. David E. Green. Grand Rapids, MI: William B. Eerdmans Publishing Company, 1977, 1998.

Botterweck, G. Johannes, Helmer Ringgren and Heinz-Josef Fabry. *Theological Dictionary of the Old Testament*, Vol. X, Trans. Douglas W. Stott. Grand Rapids, MI: William B. Eerdmans Publishing Company, 1986.

Botterweck, G. Johannes, Helmer Ringgren and Heinz-Josef Fabry. *Theological Dictionary of the Old Testament*, Vol. XI, Trans. David E. Green. Grand Rapids, MI: William B. Eerdmans Publishing Company, 2001.

Botterweck, G. Johannes, Helmer Ringgren and Heinz-Josef Fabry. *Theological Dictionary of the Old Testament*, Vol. XII, Trans. Douglas W. Stott. Grand Rapids, MI: William B. Eerdmans Publishing Company, 2003.

Botterweck, G. Johannes, Helmer Ringgren and Heinz-Josef Fabry. *Theological Dictionary of the Old Testament*, Vol. XIII, Trans. David E. Green. Grand Rapids, MI: William B. Eerdmans Publishing Company, 1977.

Botterweck, G. Johannes, Helmer Ringgren and Heinz-Josef Fabry. *Theological Dictionary of the Old Testament*, Vol. XIV, Trans.

Douglas W. Stott. Grand Rapids, MI: William B. Eerdmans Publishing Company, 2004.

Brown, Francis, S. R. Driver and Charles A. Briggs. *The Brown-Driver-Briggs Hebrew and English Lexicon*. Peabody, MA: Hendrickson, 2003.

Calvin, John. *Commentaries on the Book of Joshua,* Trans. Henry Beveridge. Grand Rapids, MI: William B. Eerdmans Publishing Company, 1949.

Chadwick, G. A. *The Book of Exodus*. New York: A. C. Armstrong and Son, 1900.

Craigie, Peter C. *Word Biblical Commentary*, Vol. 19. Waco, TX: Word Books, Publisher, 1983.

Craigie, Peter C, Page H. Kelley, and Joel F. Drinkard. *Word Biblical Commentary*, Vol. 26. Dallas, TX: Word Books, Publisher, 1991.

Cundall, Arthur E. and Leon Morris. *Judges & Ruth, An Introduction & Commentary*, Ed. D. J. Wiseman. Downers Grove, IL: InterVarsity Press, 1968.

Draper, James T. Jr. *Trusting Thy Word*. Nashville, TN: Broadman Press, 1989.

Durham, John I. *Word Biblical Commentary: Exodus,* Vol. 3, Ed. Bruce M. Metzger et al. Waco, TX: Word Books, Publisher, 1987.

Erlich, A. B. *Randglossen zur hebraischen Bibel*, Vol. V. Leipzig, 1912.

Harris, R. Laird, Gleason L. Archer, Jr., and Bruce K. Waltke. *Theological Wordbook of the Old Testament*, Vol. I. Chicago, IL: Moody Press, 1980.

Harris, R. Laird, Gleason L. Archer, Jr., and Bruce K. Waltke. *Theological Wordbook of the Old Testament*, Vol. II. Chicago, IL: Moody Press, 1980.

Hengstenberg, E. W. *The Prophecies of the Prophet Ezekiel Elucidated*, Trans. A. C. Murphy and J. G. Murphy. Minneapolis, MN: James Publications, 1976.

Holy Bible, New American Standard Bible. La Habra, CA: The Lockman Foundation, 1995.

The Holy Bible, Containing the Old and New Testaments, NKJV New King James Version. Nashville, TN: Thomas Nelson, Inc., 1988.

Kaiser, Walter C., Jr., "Exodus," *The Expositor's Bible Commentary*, Vol. 2, Ed. Frank E. Gaebelein et al. Grand Rapids, MI: Zondervan Publishing House, 1990.

Keil, C. F. and F. Delitzsch. *Commentary on the Old Testament*, Vol. I. Peabody, MA: Hendrickson Publishers, 1996.

Keil, C. F. and F. Delitzsch. *Commentary on the Old Testament in Ten Volumes*, Vol. I. Grand Rapids, MI: William B. Eerdmans Publishing Company, 1978.

Keil, C. F. and F. Delitzsch. *Commentary on the Old Testament in Ten Volumes*, Vol. I. Grand Rapids, MI: William B. Eerdmans Publishing Company, 1985.

Keil, C. F. and F. Delitzsch. *Commentary on the Old Testament in Ten Volumes*, Vol. V, Trans. James Martin. Grand Rapids, MI: William B. Eerdmans Publishing Company, 1969.

Keil, C. F. and F. Delitzsch. *Commentary on the Old Testament in Ten Volumes*, Vol. X. Grand Rapids, MI: William B. Eerdmans Publishing Company, 1984.

Lundbom, Jack R. *The Anchor Bible, Jeremiah 21-36*, Vol. 21B. New Haven, CT: Yale University Press, 2004.

Maclaren, Alexander. *The Psalms*, Vol. III, 2nd ed. New York, NY: A. C. Armstrong and Son, 1899.

Mays, James Luther. *Psalms Interpretation, A Bible Commentary for Teaching and Preaching.* Ed. James Luther Mays. Louisville, KY: John Knox Press, 1994.

Milgrom, Jacob. *The Anchor Bible, Leviticus 17-22*, Vol. 3A. New Haven, CT: Yale University Press, 2000.

Noth, Martin. *Exodus: A Commentary*, Ed. G. Ernest Wright et al. Philadelphia, PA: The Westminster Press, 1962.

Pratico, Gary D. and Miles V. Van Pelt. *Basics of Biblical Hebrew Grammar*. Grand Rapids, MI: Zondervan, 2001.

Segar, Elzie Crisler. *Popeye the Sailor*. New York, NY: King Features, A Unit of Hearst Corporation, 1933-1938.

Spurgeon, C. H. *The Treasury of David*, Vol. I, Psalm I to XXVI, 3rd Ed. New York, NY: Funk & Wagnalls Company, 1881.

Spurgeon, C. H. *The Treasury of David*, Vol. II. New York, NY: Funk & Wagnalls Company, 1870.

Spurgeon, C. H. *The Treasury of David*, Vol. VI. New York, NY: Funk & Wagnalls Company, 1881.

Strong, James. *Strong's Exhaustive Concordance of the Bible*. Iowa Falls, IA: World Bible Publishers.

Strong, James. *The Strongest Strong's Exhaustive Concordance of the Bible*. Rev. and Corr. by John R. Kohlenberger III and James A. Swanson. Grand Rapids, MI: Zondervan, 2001.

VanGemeren, Willem A. *New International Dictionary of Old Testament Theology & Exegesis,* Vol. 1. Grand Rapids, MI: Zondervan Publishing House, 1997.

VanGemeren, Willem A. *New International Dictionary of Old Testament Theology & Exegesis,* Vol. 3, Ed. Frank E. Gaebelein et al. Grand Rapids, MI: Zondervan Publishing House, 1977.

VanGemeren, Willem A. *New International Dictionary of Old Testament Theology & Exegesis,* Vol. 4, Ed. Frank E. Gaebelein et al. Grand Rapids, MI: Zondervan Publishing House, 1991.

VanGemeren, Willem A. *New International Dictionary of Old Testament Theology & Exegesis,* Vol. 5, Grand Rapids, MI: Zondervan Publishing House, 1991.

Walton, John H., Victor H. Matthews & Mark W. Chavalas. *The IVP Bible Background Commentary: Old Testament.* Downers Grove, IL: InterVarsity Press, 2000.

Wenham, Gordon J. *Word Biblical Commentary,* Vol. I, Genesis 1-15. Waco, TX: Word Books, Publisher, 1987.

William H. C. *The Anchor Bible: Exodus 1-18,* Vol. 2. New Haven, CT: Yale University Press, 1999.

Zimmerli, Walther. *A Commentary on the Book of the Prophet Ezekiel, Chapters 25-48.* Philadelphia, PA: Fortress Press, 1983.

Periodicals

Eron, Lewis John. "You Who Revere the Lord, Bless the Lord!" *Journal of Ecumenical Studies,* 18, No. 1 (Winter 1981): 63-73. *ATLA Religion Database.* EBSCOhost (16 August 2009).

Other Sources

McDonald, William. "Exodus 3:14 Devotional," Class notes from GBIB-551 Old Testament Synthesis, Oral Roberts University, September 2005.

McDonald, William. "Genesis 2:24 Devotional," Class notes from GBIB-510 Hebrew Synthesis I, Oral Roberts University, May 2007.

Newton, John. "Amazing Grace."

Revoir, James. "I'm Ugly," *Meditative Musings.* New York, NY: Authonomy.com, A Subsidiary of HarperCollins. (22 May 2011), http://authonomy.com/books/33918/meditative-musings/read-book/?chapterid=322751#chapter. (06 January 2013).

Xenophon, *The Project Gutenburg EBook of the Memorabilia, Recollections of Socrates,* Trans. H. G. Dakyns. 24 August 2008. http://www.gutenberg.org/files/1177/1177-h/1177-h.htm, (07 December 2010).

ENDNOTES

Day 1

1 Unless otherwise indicated all Bible references in this book are to the *King James Version* of the Bible.
2 Francis Brown, S. R. Driver and Charles A. Briggs, "מאד," *The Brown-Driver-Briggs Hebrew and English Lexicon*, (Peabody, MA: Hendrickson, 2003), 1033.
3 Brown, Driver, and Briggs, "מאד," 547.

Day 2

4 John H. Walton, Victor H. Matthews & Mark W. Chavalas, *The IVP Bible Background Commentary: Old Testament*, (Downers Grove, IL: InterVarsity Press, 2000), 585.
5 Brown, Driver, and Briggs, "אדם," 10.
6 Brown, Driver, and Briggs, "דם," 196.
7 Brown, Driver, and Briggs, "לבן," 526.

Day 3

8 Brown, Driver, and Briggs, "עֶלְיוֹן," 751.
9 G. Johannes Botterweck, Helmer Ringgren and Heinz-Josef Fabry, "צל," *Theological Dictionary of the Old Testament*, Vol. XII, Trans. Douglas W. Stott, (Grand Rapids, MI: William B. Eerdmans Publishing Company, 2003), 375-376.
10 Botterweck, Rinngren, and Fabry, "צל," 379.
11 Brown, Driver, and Briggs, "שַׁי," 994.
12 Brown, Driver, and Briggs, "שדי," 994.

Day 4

13 Brown, Driver, and Briggs, "ידע," 394.

Day 5

14 Brown, Driver, and Briggs, "צנה," 857.
15 Brown, Driver, and Briggs, "עטר," 742.
16 G. Johannes Botterweck, Helmer Ringgren and Heinz-Josef Fabry, "עטר," *Theological Dictionary of the Old Testament*, Vol. XI, Trans. David E. Green, (Grand Rapids, MI: William B. Eerdmans Publishing Company, 2001), 618.
17 Brown, Driver, and Briggs, "עטרה," 742.
18 Brown, Driver, and Briggs, "צן," 856.
19 Brown, Driver, and Briggs, "צנה," 856.
20 James Strong, *The Strongest Strong's Exhaustive Concordance of the Bible*, Rev. and Corr. by John R. Kohlenberger III and James A. Swanson. (Grand Rapids, MI: Zondervan, 2001), s.v. Zin, 1558.

Day 6

21 John Calvin, *Commentaries on the Book of Joshua*, Trans. Henry Beveridge, (Grand Rapids, MI: William B. Eerdmans Publishing Company, 1949), 33.
22 Brown, Driver, and Briggs, "הגה," 211.
23 G. Johannes Botterweck, Helmer Ringgren and Heinz-Josef Fabry, "צלח," *Theological Dictionary of the Old Testament*, Vol. XII, Trans. Douglas W. Stott, (Grand Rapids, MI: William B. Eerdmans Publishing Company, 2003), 384.
24 Botterweck, Rinngren, and Fabry, "צלח," 384.
25 G. Johannes Botterweck, Helmer Ringgren and Heinz-Josef Fabry, "שכל," *Theological Dictionary of the Old Testament*, Vol. XIV, Trans. Douglas W. Stott, (Grand Rapids, MI: William B. Eerdmans Publishing Company, 2004), 122.

Day 7

26 Brown, Driver, and Briggs, "קול," 877.
27 Brown, Driver, and Briggs, "רעם," 947.

28 G. Johannes Botterweck, Helmer Ringgren and Heinz-Josef Fabry, "רעם." *Theological Dictionary of the Old Testament*, Vol. XIII, Trans. David E. Green, (Grand Rapids, MI: William B. Eerdmans Publishing Company, 2004), 553.
29 C. H. Spurgeon, *The Treasury of David*, Vol. II, (New York: Funk & Wagnalls Company, 1870), 34.
30 Peter C. Craigie, *Word Biblical Commentary*, Vol. 19, (Waco, TX: Word Books, Publisher, 1983), 247.

Day 8

31 Brown, Driver, and Briggs, "כבד," 457.
32 C. F. Keil and F. Delitzsch, *Commentary on the Old Testament in Ten Volumes*, Vol. I, (Grand Rapids, MI: William B. Eerdmans Publishing Company, 1978), 122.
33 Keil and Delitzsch, 122.
34 Keil and Delitzsch, 122.
35 G. A. Chadwick, *The Book of Exodus*, (New York: A. C. Armstrong and Son, 1900), 313.

Day 9

36 Brown, Driver, and Briggs, "קדש," 872.
37 Brown, Driver, and Briggs, "בדל," 95.
38 R. Laird Harris, Gleason L. Archer, Jr., and Bruce K. Waltke, "בדל," *Theological Wordbook of the Old Testament*, Vol. I, (Chicago, IL: Moody Press, 1980), 203.
39 Jacob Milgrom, *The Anchor Bible, Leviticus 17-22*, Vol. 3A, (New Haven, CT: Yale University Press, 2000), 1762.
40 Milgrom, 1764.

Day 10

41 C. F. Keil and F. Delitzsch, *Commentary on the Old Testament*, Vol. I, (Peabody, MA: Hendrickson Publishers, 1996), 729.
42 Brown, Driver, and Briggs, "שקד,"1052.

43 Walton, Matthews, Chavalas, 643.
44 Brown, Driver, and Briggs, "שקד,"1052.

Day 11

45 Brown, Driver, and Briggs, "יצר," 427.
46 C. F. Keil and F. Delitzsch, *Commentary on the Old Testament in Ten Volumes*, Vol. I, (Grand Rapids, MI: William B. Eerdmans Publishing Company, 1985), 78.
47 Brown, Driver, and Briggs, "נפש," 659.
48 R. Laird Harris, Gleason L. Archer, Jr., and Bruce K. Waltke, "נפש," *Theological Wordbook of the Old Testament*, Vol. II, (Chicago, IL: Moody Press, 1980), 589.
49 G. Johannes Botterweck, Helmer Ringgren and Heinz-Josef Fabry, "נפש," *Theological Dictionary of the Old Testament*, Vol. IX, Trans. David E. Green, (Grand Rapids, MI: William B. Eerdmans Publishing Company, 1998), 511-512.

Day 12

50 Brown, Driver, and Briggs, "דבק," 179.
51 Willem A. VanGemeren, "דבק," *New International Dictionary of Old Testament Theology & Exegesis*, Vol. 1, (Grand Rapids, MI: Zondervan Publishing House, 1997), 911.
52 William McDonald, "Genesis 2:24 Devotional," Class notes from GBIB-510 Hebrew Synthesis I, Oral Roberts University, May 2007.
53 Gordon J. Wenham, *Word Biblical Commentary*, Vol. I, Genesis 1-15, (Waco, TX: Word Books, Publisher, 1987), 71.

Day 13

54 Arthur E. Cundall and Leon Morris, *Judges & Ruth, An Introduction & Commentary*, Ed. D. J. Wiseman, (Downers Grove, IL: Inter-Varsity Press, 1968), 159.

55 *Holy Bible, New American Standard Bible*, (La Habra, CA: The Lockman Foundation, 1995).
56 Brown, Driver, and Briggs, "פלאי," 811.
57 Brown, Driver, and Briggs, "פלא," 810.
58 Brown, Driver, and Briggs, "פלג," 811.
59 G. Johannes Botterweck, Helmer Ringgren and Heinz-Josef Fabry, "פלא," *Theological Dictionary of the Old Testament*, Vol. XI, Trans. David E. Green, (Grand Rapids, MI: William B. Eerdmans Publishing Company, 2001), 535.

Day 14

60 Brown, Driver, and Briggs, "נֵר," 632.
61 G. Johannes Botterweck, Helmer Ringgren and Heinz-Josef Fabry, "נֵר," *Theological Dictionary of the Old Testament*, Vol. X, Trans. Douglas W. Stott, (Grand Rapids, MI: William B. Eerdmans Publishing Company, 1986), 20.
62 Botterweck, Ringgren and Fabry, "נֵר," 20.
63 Botterweck, Ringgren and Fabry, "נֵר," 20.
64 Botterweck, Ringgren and Fabry, "נֵר," 20.
65 C. H. Spurgeon, *The Treasury of David*, Vol. VI, (New York, NY: Funk & Wagnalls Company, 1881), 243.
66 Brown, Driver, and Briggs, "אוֹר," 21.
67 G. Johannes Botterweck and Helmer Ringgren, "אוֹר," *Theological Dictionary of the Old Testament*, Vol. I, Trans. John T. Willis, (Grand Rapids, MI: William B. Eerdmans Publishing Company, 1977), 151.
68 James T. Draper Jr., *Trusting Thy Word*, (Nashville, TN: Broadman Press, 1989), 136.

Day 15

69 G. Johannes Botterweck and Helmer Ringgren, "ירא," *Theological Dictionary of the Old Testament*, Vol. VI, Trans. David E. Green, (Grand Rapids, MI: William B. Eerdmans Publishing Company, 1990), 295.
70 Botterweck and Ringgren, "ירא," 290.

71 Brown, Driver, and Briggs, "ירא," 431.
72 Lewis John Eron, "You Who Revere the Lord, Bless the Lord!" *Journal of Ecumenical Studies*, 18, No. 1 (Winter 1981): 67. *ATLA Religion Database*. EBSCOhost (16 August 2009).
73 Eron, 68.

Day 16

74 C. F. Keil and F. Delitzsch, *Commentary on the Old Testament in Ten Volumes*, Vol. X, (Grand Rapids, MI: William B. Eerdmans Publishing Company, 1984), 160.
75 Brown, Driver, and Briggs, "שׂישׂ," 965.
76 Brown, Driver, and Briggs, "שׂמחה," 970.
77 Brown, Driver, and Briggs, "שׂמח," 970.
78 Brown, Driver, and Briggs, "גיל," 162.
79 Brown, Driver, and Briggs, "גיל," 162.
80 G. Johannes Botterweck and Helmer Ringgren, "גיל," *Theological Dictionary of the Old Testament*, Vol. II, Trans. John T. Willis, (Grand Rapids, MI: William B. Eerdmans Publishing Company, 1975), 473.
81 Brown, Driver, and Briggs, "רנה," 943.
82 Brown, Driver, and Briggs, "חרשׂ," 361.
83 Keil and Delitzsch, 161.

Day 17

84 Brown, Driver, and Briggs, "גבר," 149.
85 G. Johannes Botterweck and Helmer Ringgren, "גבר," *Theological Dictionary of the Old Testament*, Vol. II, Trans. John T. Willis, (Grand Rapids, MI: William B. Eerdmans Publishing Company, 1975), 369-373.
86 Botterweck and Ringgren, "גבר," 370.
87 Botterweck and Ringgren, "גבר," 370.
88 Botterweck and Ringgren, "גבר," 372.
89 Botterweck and Ringgren, "גבר," 373.
90 Botterweck and Ringgren, "גבר," 374.

91 John H. Walton, Victor H. Matthews & Mark W. Chavalas, *The IVP Bible Background Commentary: Old Testament*, (Downers Grove, IL: InterVarsity Press, 2000), 525.

Day 18

92 Brown, Driver, and Briggs, "ישע," 446.
93 Brown, Driver, and Briggs, "ישע," 446-447.

Day 19

94 R. Laird Harris, Gleason L. Archer, Jr., and Bruce K. Waltke, "שלום," *Theological Wordbook of the Old Testament*, Vol. II, (Chicago, IL: Moody Press, 1980), 931.
95 Harris, Archer, and Waltke, "שלום," 931.
96 Brown, Driver, and Briggs, "שלום," 1022.
97 Brown, Driver, and Briggs, "שלום," 1022.
98 Harris, Archer, and Waltke, "שלום," 931.

Day 20

99 Brown, Driver, and Briggs, "חשב," 363.
100 R. Laird Harris, Gleason L. Archer, Jr., and Bruce K. Waltke, "חשב," *Theological Wordbook of the Old Testament*, Vol. I, (Chicago, IL: Moody Press, 1980), 768.
101 Brown, Driver, and Briggs, "תקוה," 876.
102 Brown, Driver, and Briggs, "תקוה," 876.
103 Brown, Driver, and Briggs, "קוה," 875.
104 G. Johannes Botterweck, Helmer Ringgren and Heinz-Josef Fabry, "קוה," *Theological Dictionary of the Old Testament*, Vol. XII, Trans. Douglas W. Stott, (Grand Rapids, MI: William B. Eerdmans Publishing Company, 2003), 571.
105 Botterweck, Ringgren and Fabry, "קוה," 571.
106 Judah, 155.

Day 21

[107] Brown, Driver, and Briggs, "חסידה," 339.
[108] Brown, Driver, and Briggs, "חסד," 338.
[109] Willem A. VanGemeren, "Psalms," *The Expositor's Bible Commentary*, Vol. 5, Ed. Frank E. Gaebelein et al. (Grand Rapids, MI: Zondervan Publishing House, 1991), 823.
[110] VanGemeren, 824.
[111] VanGemeren, 825.
[112] VanGemeren, 825.
[113] J. Zobel, "חסד," *Theological Dictionary of the Old Testament*, Vol. V, Ed. G. Johannes Botterweck and Helmer Ringgren, Trans. David E. Green, (Grand Rapids, MI: William B. Eerdmans Publishing Company, 1986), 62.
[114] Zobel, 51.

Day 22

[115] Brown, Driver, and Briggs, "היה," 224.
[116] James Strong, "Nave's Topical Bible Reference System," in *The Strongest Strong's Exhaustive Concordance of the Bible*, Rev. and Corr. by John R. Kohlenberger III and James A. Swanson. (Grand Rapids, MI: Zondervan, 2001), s.v. Jehovah, 1733.
[117] William McDonald, "Exodus 3:14 Devotional," Class notes from GBIB-551 Old Testament Synthesis, Oral Roberts University, (September 2005).
[118] William H. C. Propp, *The Anchor Bible: Exodus 1-18,* Vol. 2, (New Haven, CT: Yale University Press, 1999), 205.
[119] James Strong, *The Strongest Strong's Exhaustive Concordance of the Bible,* Rev. and Corr. by John R. Kohlenberger III and James A. Swanson. (Grand Rapids, MI: Zondervan, 2001), 1508.
[120] Durham, 39.
[121] J. F. McLaughlin, "Exodus," *The Abingdon Bible Commentary*, Ed. Frederick Carl Eiselen et al. (New York, NY: Abingdon Press, 1929), 256.

[122] Walter C. Kaiser, Jr., "Exodus," *The Expositor's Bible Commentary*, Vol. 2, Ed. Frank E. Gaebelein et al. (Grand Rapids, MI: Zondervan Publishing House, 1990), 321.
[123] Kaiser 321.
[124] Kaiser 321.

Day 23

[125] Brown, Driver, and Briggs, "ראה," 906.
[126] R. Laird Harris, Gleason L. Archer, Jr., and Bruce K. Waltke, "ראה," *Theological Wordbook of the Old Testament*, Vol. II, (Chicago, IL: Moody Press, 1980), 823.
[127] *The Holy Bible, Containing the Old and New Testaments, NKJV New King James Version*, (Nashville, TN: Thomas Nelson, Inc., 1988).

Day 24

[128] Brown, Driver, and Briggs, "רפא," 950.
[129] Brown, Driver, and Briggs, "רפא," 950.
[130] G. Johannes Botterweck, Helmer Ringgren and Heinz-Josef Fabry, "רפא," *Theological Dictionary of the Old Testament*, Vol. XIII, Trans. David E. Green, (Grand Rapids, MI: William B. Eerdmans Publishing Company, 1977), 597; A. B. Erlich, *Randglossen zur hebraischen Bibel*, Vol. V, (Leipzig, 1912), 200.

Day 25

[131] Brown, Driver, and Briggs, "שמ," 1027.
[132] Gary D. Pratico and Miles V. Van Pelt, *Basics of Biblical Hebrew Grammar*, (Grand Rapids, MI: Zondervan, 2001), 71.
[133] Brown, Driver, and Briggs, "עמנו אל," 769.
[134] Brown, Driver, and Briggs, "עמנו אל," 769.
[135] Brown, Driver, and Briggs, "עמנו אל," 769.

Day 26

[136] John H. Walton, Victor H. Matthews & Mark W. Chavalas, *The IVP Bible Background Commentary: Old Testament*, (Downers Grove, IL: InterVarsity Press, 2000), 93.

[137] Brown, Driver, and Briggs, "נס," 651.

[138] Brown, Driver, and Briggs, "נסס," 651.

[139] R. Laird Harris, Gleason L. Archer, Jr., and Bruce K. Waltke, "נס," *Theological Wordbook of the Old Testament*, Vol. II, (Chicago, IL: Moody Press, 1980), 583.

[140] G. Johannes Botterweck, Helmer Ringgren and Heinz-Josef Fabry, "נס," *Theological Dictionary of the Old Testament*, Vol. IX, Trans. David E. Green, (Grand Rapids, MI: William B. Eerdmans Publishing Company, 1977), 440.

[141] Botterweck, Ringgren and Fabry, "נס," 440.

[142] Martin Noth, *Exodus: A Commentary*, Ed. G. Ernest Wright et al., (Philadelphia, PA: The Westminster Press, 1962), 144.

[143] Botterweck, Ringgren and Fabry, "נס," 440.

[144] Botterweck, Ringgren and Fabry, "נס," 440.

[145] R. Laird Harris, Gleason L. Archer, Jr., and Bruce K. Waltke, "נסס," *Theological Wordbook of the Old Testament*, Vol. II, (Chicago, IL: Moody Press, 1980), 583.

Day 27

[146] Brown, Driver, and Briggs, "צבא," 838.

[147] Brown, Driver, and Briggs, "צבא," 838.

Day 28

[148] James Strong, "Nave's Topical Bible Reference System," in *The Strongest Strong's Exhaustive Concordance of the Bible*, Rev. and Corr. by John R. Kohlenberger III and James A. Swanson. (Grand Rapids, MI: Zondervan, 2001), s.v. Yahweh Tsidkenu, 1714.

[149] Peter C. Craigie, Page H. Kelley, and Joel J. Drinkard, *Word Biblical Commentary*, Vol. 26, Jeremiah 1-25, (Dallas, TX: Word Books, Publisher, 1991), xlv.
[150] Brown, Driver, and Briggs, "עדה," 723.
[151] G. Johannes Botterweck, Helmer Ringgren and Heinz-Josef Fabry, "צדק," *Theological Dictionary of the Old Testament*, Vol. XII, Trans. Douglas W. Stott, (Grand Rapids, MI: William B. Eerdmans Publishing Company, 2003), 254.
[152] Jack R. Lundbom, *The Anchor Bible, Jeremiah 21-.36*, Vol. 21B, (New Haven, CT: Yale University Press, 2004), 175.
[153] Brown, Driver, and Briggs, "צדק," 842.

Day 29

[154] Brown, Driver, and Briggs, "ברית," 136.
[155] Willem A. VanGemeren, "ברית," *New International Dictionary of Old Testament Theology & Exegesis*, Vol. 1, (Grand Rapids, MI: Zondervan Publishing House, 1997), 747.
[156] G. Johannes Botterweck and Helmer Ringgren, "ברית," *Theological Dictionary of the Old Testament*, Vol. II, Trans. John T. Willis, (Grand Rapids, MI: William B. Eerdmans Publishing Company, 1975), 253.
[157] Botterweck and Ringgren, "ברית," 254.
[158] Botterweck and Ringgren, "ברית," 255.
[159] Botterweck and Ringgren, "ברית," 255.
[160] VanGemeren, "ברית," 747.
[161] VanGemeren, "ברית," 747.
[162] Botterweck and Ringgren, "ברר," 140.
[163] VanGemeren, "ברית," 747.

Day 30

[164] Brown, Driver, and Briggs, "סגלה," 688.
[165] James Revoir, "I'm Ugly," *Meditative Musings*, (New York, NY: Authonomy.com, A Subsidiary of HarperCollins), (22 May 2011)

http://authonomy.com/books/33918/meditative-musings/read-book/?chapterid=322751#chapter (06 January 2013).

Day 31

[166] Brown, Driver, and Briggs, "דשׁן," 206.
[167] G. Johannes Botterweck and Helmer Ringgren, "דשׁן," *Theological Dictionary of the Old Testament*, Vol. III, Trans. John T. Willis and Geoffrey W. Bromiley, (Grand Rapids, MI: William B. Eerdmans Publishing Company, 1978), 311.

Day 32

[168] Elzie Crisler Segar, *Popeye the Sailor,* (New York, NY: King Features, A Unit of Hearst Corporation), 1933-1938.
[169] Brown, Driver, and Briggs, "זית," 268.
[170] G. Johannes Botterweck and Helmer Ringgren, "זית," *Theological Dictionary of the Old Testament*, Vol. IV, Trans. David E. Green, (Grand Rapids, MI: William B. Eerdmans Publishing Company, 1980), 59.
[171] Botterweck and Ringgren, "זית,"59.
[172] Botterweck and Ringgren, "זית,"59.
[173] Botterweck and Ringgren, "זית," 59.
[174] Botterweck and Ringgren, "זית," 59.
[175] Botterweck and Ringgren, "זית,"59.

Day 33

[176] Kay Arthur, *The New Inductive Study Bible*, (Eugene, OR: Precept Ministries International, Published by Harvest House Publishers, 2000), 1321.
[177] Arthur, 1321.
[178] Brown, Driver, and Briggs, "רמשׂ," 943.
[179] Brown, Driver, and Briggs, "שׁקץ," 1055.

180 E. W. Hengstenberg, *The Prophecies of the Prophet Ezekiel Elucidated*, Trans. A. C. Murphy and J. G. Murphy, (Minneapolis, MN: James Publications, 1976), 76.

Day 34

181 Brown, Driver, and Briggs, "רפה," 951.
182 Brown, Driver, and Briggs, "עזב," 736.

Day 35

183 Brown, Driver, and Briggs, "הלל," 237.
184 Brown, Driver, and Briggs, "הלל," 237.
185 John Newton, "Amazing Grace."
186 Leslie C. Allen, "הלל," *New International Dictionary of Old Testament Theology & Exegesis*, Vol. 1, Ed. Willem A. VanGemeren, (Grand Rapids, MI: Zondervan Publishing House, 1997), 1035.
187 Allen, 1035.
188 Helmer Ringgren, "הלל," *Theological Dictionary of the Old Testament*, Vol. III, Ed. G. Johannes Botterweck and Helmer Ringgren, Trans. John T. Willis and Geoffrey W. Bromiley, (Grand Rapids, MI: William B. Eerdmans Publishing Company, 1978), 404.
189 Helmer Ringgren, 404.
190 James Luther Mays, *Psalms Interpretation, A Bible Commentary for Teaching and Preaching*, Ed. James Luther Mays, (Louisville, KY: John Knox Press, 1994), 451.

Day 36

191 Brown, Driver, and Briggs, "קנא," 888.
192 Brown, Driver, and Briggs, "קנא," 888.
193 Nahum M. Sarna, *The JPS Torah Commentary*: *Exodus*, (Philadelphia, PA: The Jewish Publication Society, 1991), 110.
194 Brown, Driver, and Briggs, "קנא," 888.

195 Brown, Driver, and Briggs, "קנא," 888.
196 R. Laird Harris, Gleason L. Archer, Jr., and Bruce K. Waltke, "קנא," *Theological Wordbook of the Old Testament*, Vol. II, (Chicago, IL: Moody Press, 1980), 802.

Day 37

197 Walther Zimmerli, *A Commentary on the Book of the Prophet Ezekiel, Chapters 25-48*, (Philadelphia, PA: Fortress Press, 1983), 249.
198 Brown, Driver, and Briggs, "זרק," 284.
199 Brown, Driver, and Briggs, "נזה," 633.
200 Daniel I. Block, *The Book of Ezekiel, Chapters 25-48*, (Grand Rapids, MI: William B. Eerdmans Publishing Company, 1997), 354-355.
201 Brown, Driver, and Briggs, "טהר," 372.
202 Helmer Ringgren, "טהר," *Theological Dictionary of the Old Testament*, Vol. V, Ed. G. Johannes Botterweck and Helmer Ringgren, Trans. David E. Green, (Grand Rapids, MI: William B. Eerdmans Publishing Company, 1986), 290.
203 Ringgren, "טהר," 290.

Day 38

204 Brown, Driver, and Briggs, "חלי," 318.
205 Brown, Driver, and Briggs, "חלה," 317.
206 Brown, Driver, and Briggs, "מכאוב," 456.
207 Brown, Driver, and Briggs, "מכאוב," 456.
208 R. Mosis, "כאב," *Theological Dictionary of the Old Testament*, Vol. VII, Ed. G. Johannes Botterweck, Helmer Ringgren and Heinz-Josef Fabry, Trans. David E. Green, (Grand Rapids, MI: William B. Eerdmans Publishing Company, 1995), 9.
209 Mosis, "כאב," 10.
210 Brown, Driver, and Briggs, "סבל," 687.
211 Brown, Driver, and Briggs, "סבל," 688.

Day 39

[212] C. F. Keil and F. Delitzsch, *Commentary on the Old Testament*, Vol. I, (Peabody, MA: Hendrickson Publishers, 1996), 79.
[213] Keil and Delitzsch, *Commentary on the Old Testament*, Vol. I, 79.
[214] Nahum M. Sarna, *The JPS Torah Commentary*: *Genesis*, (Philadelphia, PA: The Jewish Publication Society, 1998), 43.
[215] Brown, Driver, and Briggs, "הלך," 229.
[216] Brown, Driver, and Briggs, "הלך," 236.
[217] Sarna, 43.
[218] F. J. Helfmeyer, "הלך," *Theological Dictionary of the Old Testament*, Vol. III, Ed. G. Johannes Botterweck and Helmer Ringgren, Trans. John T. Willis, Geoffrey W. Bromiley and David E. Green, (Grand Rapids, MI: William B. Eerdmans Publishing Company, 1978), 389.
[219] Helfmeyer, "הלך," 391.
[220] Keil and Delitzsch, *Commentary on the Old Testament*, Vol. I, 79.

Day 40

[221] Brown, Driver, and Briggs, "סוֹד," 691.
[222] Heinz-Josef Fabry, "סוֹד." *Theological Dictionary of the Old Testament*, Vol. X, Trans. Douglas W. Stott, (Grand Rapids, MI: William B. Eerdmans Publishing Company, 1986), 172.
[223] Brown, Driver, and Briggs, "יסד" 413.
[224] C. F. Keil and F. Delitzsch, *Commentary on the Old Testament in Ten Volumes*, Vol. V, Trans. James Martin, (Grand Rapids, MI: William B. Eerdmans Publishing Company, 1969), 345.
[225] C. H. Spurgeon, *The Treasury of David*, Vol. I, Psalm I to XXVI, 3rd Ed., (New York, NY: Funk & Wagnalls Company, 1881), 446.
[226] Spurgeon, 446.

Day 41

[227] Brown, Driver, and Briggs, "עזר," 740.

228 G. Johannes Botterweck, Helmer Ringgren and Heinz-Josef Fabry, "נָגַד," *Theological Dictionary of the Old Testament*, Vol. IX, Trans. David E. Green, (Grand Rapids, MI: William B. Eerdmans Publishing Company, 1998), 175.
229 Brown, Driver, and Briggs, "נגד," 616.
230 C. F. Keil and F. Delitzsch, *Commentary on the Old Testament in Ten Volumes*, Vol. I, (Grand Rapids, MI: William B. Eerdmans Publishing Company, 1978), 90.
231 Brown, Driver, and Briggs, "אדם," 9.
232 Brown, Driver, and Briggs, "עשׂה," 61.
233 Brown, Driver, and Briggs, "אישׁ," 35.
234 Nahum M. Sarna, *The JPS Torah Commentary: Genesis*, (Philadelphia, PA: The Jewish Publication Society, 1998), 23.

Day 42

235 C. H. Spurgeon, *The Treasury of David*, Vol. I, (New York, NY: Funk & Wagnalls Company, 1881), 253.
236 Xenophon, *The Project Gutenburg EBook of the Memorabilia, Recollections of Socrates,* Trans. H. G. Dakyns. 24 August 2008. http://www.gutenberg.org/files/1177/1177-h/1177-h.htm, (07 December 2010).
237 Brown, Driver, and Briggs, "בבה," 93.
238 Brown, Driver, and Briggs, "נבב," 612.
239 Brown, Driver, and Briggs, "בבה," 93.
240 Brown, Driver, and Briggs, "בת," 123.

www.ingramcontent.com/pod-product-compliance
Lightning Source LLC
Chambersburg PA
CBHW062200080426
42734CB00010B/1755